SOCIAL
STUDIES
SOURCES

Erling M. Hunt, Series Editor

**Congress and the President:
Readings in Executive-Legislative Relations**
by Walter Earl Travis

A Bibliography for Teachers of Social Studies
by Raymond A. Ducharme, Jr., Joseph Katz, and
Arthur D. Sheekey

Honors Teaching in American History
by Lawrence A. Fink

American History Through Conflicting Interpretations
by David F. Kellum

Charles A. Beard and the Social Studies: A Book of Readings
by Raymond A. Ducharme, Jr.

HONORS TEACHING IN AMERICAN HISTORY

LAWRENCE A. FINK

Social Studies Sources
Erling M. Hunt, Series Editor

Teachers College Press
Teachers College, Columbia University
New York, New York

Foreword

Effective teaching of American history in secondary schools has faced two obstacles that it has rarely surmounted. First, that it is usually the third presentation of our national history and that it usually adds little to the junior-high-school cycle has deprived it of freshness. Second, textbooks that survey ever-expanding American history have had to confine their accounts to surface narrative of events. Authors and teachers alike, trapped by limitations of space and time, have focused on teaching facts.

The freshness of American history in secondary schools lies in its primary sources—documents and firsthand accounts. Its challenge to good minds—and perhaps to most minds—lies in evaluation of those sources, in the conclusions that such study suggests, and in consideration of the differing conclusions that historians have advanced from fuller and deeper study of sources.

Dr. Fink, with a class of high-ability students, demonstrated the challenge of primary sources and the response of good minds to them. The sources are readily available and so were better than average resources for following up questions and issues identified by the students. Even without all those resources, there can be student thought, discussion, insight, and new enthusiasm for studying American history. Even with sacrifice of full coverage, learning facts was no problem—the students learned them when they needed them, and passed state and nation-wide exams with distinction.

Teachers can readily adapt the use of sources for other high-ability classes. There is increasing evidence, moreover, that "average" students also respond to the freshness of sources and the challenge of an opportunity to formulate and discuss their own ideas of our past. The flood of source publications, many in paperback, makes possible, as Dr. Fink has shown, an end to perfunctory teaching and study of American history.

Erling M. Hunt

May 1969

Preface

America in the late 1960's has been labeled a "sick society." The unlicensed social physicians often include in their diagnosis a weakness in the teaching of American history. Other practitioners overreact to some ultra-patriotic presentations of American history and assert that the true history of the United States is a dark one. The disillusionment of many of our young people comes from many sources—an unpopular war, a violent domestic environment, and a suffocation of affluence. To be patriotic in some circles is almost to be subversive. A small segment of the student population is sworn to disrupt and destroy American society. Our colleges and universities and all symbols of authority are the enemy.

One possible remedy for the current school population—it is too late for their older brothers and sisters—might be to allow them some latitude in interpreting our past history for themselves. Proper use of primary source materials could be one way of helping our young people come to some conclusions. One approach is described in the following pages. This presentation applies to academically talented high school students. Adjustments in selection of sources and format can be made for the use of young people of differing ability levels.

American history is generally taught to our young citizens in the fifth grade, in the eighth grade, and again in the eleventh or twelfth grade. Those going on to college are often exposed to still another survey and a variety of period or topical courses. Some differentiation of approach and materials should be made but quite often is not. While criticism of the ideas and proposals presented herein must and should be directed at the author, there are several friends and colleagues who have been most gracious in sharing their thoughts on the teaching of American history: Raymond A. Ducharme, Jr., Joseph Katz, Stanley M. Elkins, and Donald H. Sheehan. F. Loretta Coons, Erling Hunt, and Cliff Bragdon must be keenly aware of the debt owed to them. Finally, I thank the best teacher I have ever known, Barbara L. Fink.

Lawrence A. Fink

Northampton, Massachusetts
April 1969

Contents

Honors Teaching in American History

One: The Challenge and Promise of Honors Courses

American history as taught in American high schools needs vitalizing. Usually it is not the stimulating, challenging, and exciting subject it should be. The great majority of American history courses are built around a textbook narrative, written with a national market in mind, requiring little more than recall of innumerable "facts." More profitable and stimulating would be an American history course that drew on primary sources and on varying and changing interpretations.

There are some encouraging recent developments in the teaching of history. Salary schedules increasingly encourage and recognize graduate study beyond minimum certification requirements. Some high school textbooks have moved beyond narrative surveys to more interpretive treatment of movements and of social policies, and some such volumes previously used exclusively at the college level have found their way into high school classes. The growth of the Advanced Placement Program has brought about some improvement in secondary school offerings for the more able students by providing a reason and a means for introducing college level courses. Library resources continue to grow as state departments of education require high schools to employ trained librarians and meet at least minimum standards, and as more and more new volumes, both hard cover and paperback, are published. The National Council for the Social Studies Yearbooks on American history are particularly valuable, especially the thirty-first yearbook, *Interpreting and Teaching American History*.[1] The American Historical Association's Service Center for Teachers of History prepares an ever-growing series of pamphlets on specific fields of history designed to keep the classroom teacher informed on the latest scholarship and interpretations. In some public schools the answer to the needs of able students has been the development of special classes, often called honors classes, which allow for a course of study differen-

[1] William H. Cartwright and Richard L. Watson, Jr. (co-editors), *Interpreting and Teaching American History* (Washington, D.C.: National Council for the Social Studies, 1961, 430 pp.).

1

tiated from that offered to other college preparatory students. Actual differences, however, do not always exist.

THE DEVELOPMENT OF THE HIGH SCHOOL COURSE: A HISTORICAL PERSPECTIVE

Textbooks in American history began to appear in the United States immediately after the establishment of the federal union. The primary reasons were nationalism and democracy. There was an immediate move to direct the loyalty of the youth to the new nation rather than to the state or section and authors, in addition, were also conscious of the Jeffersonian ideal of an educated electorate as necessary for the operation of democracy. In 1827, both Massachusetts and Vermont mandated the teaching of United States history in all towns within their boundaries. From 1870 on, a growing number of colleges added history to their formal entrance requirements.

As American education developed during the nineteenth century, three cycles of teaching the history of the United States were established. Early in the development, the first cycle was placed in the elementary school so that students would be exposed to the history of their country before they left the schoolhouse. As students began to remain in school through the eighth grade, a second cycle of American history was included in the curriculum of that grade to expose the students immediately before they left school. Finally, when high schools expanded in number and scope, a third cycle was introduced. As each course was added, none was removed from the earlier grade levels, so that in most school systems today in the United States, students go through three cycles of American history before they graduate from high school.

SHAPING THE HIGH SCHOOL COURSE

The high school American history course was at first developed in accordance with what was written in available textbooks. The books were written by authors and used by teachers with no professional preparation. There were no professors of history and no major in history was offered in the nation's colleges. The American Historical Association was founded in 1884 with but nine members.

To bring some order into the confusion of secondary school curricula, the National Education Association created in 1892 the Committee of Ten, of which a subcommittee held a Conference on History, Civil Government, and Political Economy at Madison in 1893. The Conference resulted in recommendations which included four years of high school history, of which one should be American.[2] In a second and

[2] National Education Association, *Report of the Committee of Ten on Sec-*

more successful effort to reduce curriculum chaos, the American Historical Association created its Committee of Seven in 1896; its 1899 report recommended that the high school curriculum should include a study of ancient history the first year; medieval and modern European history the second year; English history the third year; and American history and civil government the fourth year.[3] In part because the College Entrance Examination Board, established in 1900, adopted the Committee of Seven report as the pattern for its examinations, American history became standard throughout the nation as a twelfth grade course.

Meanwhile, history was established as a major field of study in colleges, and the *History Teacher's Magazine* appeared in 1909. Professional historians began to write textbooks for high school courses and teach prospective history teachers. In 1911 David Saville Muzzey wrote a textbook that shifted the midpoint of high school American history from 1783 to 1865. In 1912 James Harvey Robinson published his *New History* which advocated less attention to political, constitutional, and military aspects of history and more attention to social, cultural, and economic development.

Other factors affecting secondary schools and the place of American history in them became apparent in the early part of the twentieth century. Increased enrollments brought many youths for whom traditional courses were inappropriate or inadequate. The new psychology of G. Stanley Hall, William James, and Edward L. Thorndike and the philosophy of John Dewey changed pedagogical theory and influenced an ever-growing number of methods courses and methods texts, including those in the teaching of history. The Progressives, demanding social reforms, influenced many school leaders. The social sciences—political science, economics, sociology—sought recognition in secondary schools. Normal-school professors, school superintendents and principals, and classroom teachers called for curriculum reform.

The American Historical Association, in response to rising discontent, appointed a Committee of Five to review the 1899 report. The new committee missed its opportunity; it recommended virtually no change from the suggestions of the Committee of Seven. In so doing it allowed curriculum leadership to pass to professional educators, and it was not until the 1916 report of the Committee on the Social Studies, established by the N. E. A. Commission on the Reorganization of Secondary

---

ondary School Subjects . . . with the reports of the conferences . . . , Washington, D. C.: N. E. A., 1893, pp. 46–47.

3 American Historical Association, *The Study of History in Schools, Report to the American Historical Association by the Committee of Seven* (New York: The Macmillan Company, 1899), pp. 34–35.

Education, that the new forces and demands were reflected.[4] In 1920, the recommendation was drastically applied by Charles and Mary Beard; a little more than a decade later, textbooks by Faulkner and Kepner and by F. P. Wirth adopted topical-unit organizations. The content and organization of these texts attempted partially to make some provision for the able high school student, who had been somewhat forgotten as educators responded to a changing high school population.

A CONFUSION IN AIMS

There is a lack in the educational literature of clearly focused aims for social studies instruction. The teacher not guilty of adopting the single aim of transmitting factual data by rote memorization tends instead to lose focus, taking into account a multitude of stated objectives, which, in categories of information, understandings, skills, attitudes, and behavior, sometimes numbers into the hundreds. Moreover, the elementary, junior high, and senior high schools cannot seem to establish distinctive aims for successive cycles of the American history course.

Henry Johnson has maintained that the controlling purpose of American history is the understanding of the social and political world around us through the teaching of developmental history and the concomitant skill of the critical method.[5] Such an objective could never be fulfilled within the format of most current classroom operations. *A Charter for the Social Sciences in the Schools,* drafted by Charles Beard, identifies three factors that inescapably condition what is taught in the social sciences: the necessities of scholarship, the realities of society, and the requirements of the teaching and learning process.[6] Beard analyzed the social understanding for which Johnson had called and endorsed Johnson's emphasis on critical method: "A knowledge of how to acquire knowledge is a permanent possession which can be used throughout life."[7]

[4] *Report of the Committee on the Social Studies . . . ,* U. S. Bureau of Education Bulletin No. 28 (Washington, D. C.: U. S. Bureau of Education, 1916); *Preliminary Statements by Chairmen of Committees of the Commission of the National Education Association on the Reorganization of Secondary Education,* U. S. Bureau of Education Bulletin No. 41 (Washington, D. C.: U. S. Bureau of Education, 1916). It should be noted that the report recognized social studies other than history.
[5] Henry Johnson, *Teaching of History in Elementary and Secondary Schools with Applications to Allied Studies* (New York: The Macmillan Company, 1940), p. 108ff.
[6] Charles A. Beard, *A Charter for the Social Sciences in the Schools* (New York: Charles Scribner's Sons, 1932), p. 3. The *Charter* is the first in the seventeen volumes published by the American Historical Association's Commission on the Social Studies.
[7] Ibid., p. 99.

If one accepts these ideas, then it becomes necessary to set about adopting different approaches to the teaching of American history. Not only should there be distinctive aims for the successive cycles of American history but differentiation should also be made for varying levels of ability: an honors course for academically able youth should include work with source materials and interpretations—the tools and the product of the historian. Although the views of Johnson and Beard were published between 1915 and 1934,[8] their ideas are yet to be heeded by more than a handful of teachers and administrators.

A HISTORY OF PROGRAMS FOR ABLE STUDENTS

Although the small secondary school population remained until the end of the nineteenth century a select segment of their age group, the question of what kind of history was appropriate to their abilities received little attention.

A source method in history that closely parallels the method in the honors class described in later chapters was developed in the 1880's and 1890's by Mary Sheldon Barnes. The Report of the Committee of Seven deals primarily with the college preparatory student and his program, for which Mrs. Barnes's source method now seems appropriate. But the Committee, though interested in some use of sources, declared that they "are not intended to be either the sole or the principal materials for school study."[9] Three years later, a case was made for using original source materials in all history courses.[10]

Many publications, some intended for use in secondary schools, made selected source materials available to teachers and students.[11] The volume by Nevins and Commager, *The Heritage of America,* and Commager's *Documents of American History* are representative of many

[8] Henry Johnson's *Teaching of History* first appeared in 1915.

[9] *Report to the American Historical Association by the Committee of Seven* (New York: The Macmillan Company, 1906), p. 103.

[10] New England History Teachers' Association, *Historical Sources in Schools, Report . . . A Select Committee* (New York: The Macmillan Company, 1902), 299 pp.

[11] Albert Bushnell Hart and Edward Channing (editors), *American History Leaflets* (New York: Lovell and Company, 1892–1902), 34 nos.

Edwin Doak Mead (editor), *Old South Leaflets* (Boston: Directors of the Old South Work, 1883–1901), 125 nos.

Albert Bushnell Hart (editor), *American History as Told by Contemporaries* (New York: The Macmillan Company, 1897–1929), 5 vols. Each volume indexed and sold separately.

A. C. McLaughlin, W. E. Dodd, M. W. Jernegan and A. P. Scott (editors), *Source Problems in United States History* (New York: Harper and Brothers, 1918), 514 pp.

publications that testify to some continuing conviction that primary sources have a role in history teaching. Few teachers, however, could spare time from textbook teaching for such luxuries.

HIGH IQ, LOW EXPECTATION

The use of intelligence tests and related classifications of the school population in the first two decades of the twentieth century, the special concern for the gifted of such psychologists as Professors Lewis Terman and Leta S. Hollingworth, brought little change in history teaching. Differentiation in American history, usually required for all seniors or juniors, occurred only as college preparatory sections tended to include abler youth, some of whom would take College Board tests, and as more experienced or more effective teachers might be assigned to eleventh or twelfth grade classes. The College Entrance Examination Board's tests in history set essay questions until the later 1930's,[12] and "thought questions," calling for comparison, contrasts, and analysis, promptly became subjects for drill in the classes of sophisticated teachers who specialized in preparing college-bound youth for the CEEB examinations. Private or independent schools followed the lead of college preparatory history sections in public high schools. Any relative advantages enjoyed by high prestige schools were reflections of their selectivity, together with freedom from public school commitment to "equality of opportunity," identified by many theorists and practitioners with identity of experience.

Schools, both public and private, lacked the theory and practical principles for differentiating elementary from advanced history. Any notable challenge to high ability reflected the personality, the power, or some unusual practice of an exceptional teacher. The clues to the nature of advanced history provided in Henry Johnson's analysis were usually ignored, or perhaps not understood.

The *New York Times* campaign, in the early 1940's, for more American history in schools and colleges stressed quantity rather than quality.[13] One report did, however, sharply criticize the undifferentiated and unstimulating repetition that characterized the successive cycles of American history in schools and colleges.[14] However, its recommen-

---

[12] Harriet H. Shoen, *The History Examinations of the College Entrance Examination Board* (New York: The author, 1944).

[13] Allan Nevins, "American History for Americans," *New York Times Magazine* (May 3, 1942), p. 14; *New York Times* (April 4, 1943); Erling M. Hunt, "More American History?" *Social Education, 6* (October 1942), p. 250; Erling M. Hunt, "The *New York Times* 'Test' on American History," *Social Education, 7* (May 1943), pp. 195–200.

[14] Edgar B. Wesley (Director), *American History in Schools and Colleges:* Report of the Committee on American History in Schools and Colleges of the American Historical Association, The Mississippi Valley Historical Associa-

dations for differentiating emphasis according to chronological periods had no influence on actual practice.

DIFFERENTIATED PROGRAMS FOR THE GIFTED

American educators have long been concerned with the academic development of their very able students, and as the range of ability among high school youth has widened, a controversy has developed concerning the efficacy of homogeneous grouping as opposed to hetero- geneous grouping. Even among the proponents of homogeneous group- ing there has remained a widespread conviction that grouping for the social studies should remain heterogeneous so that the subject can continue to exert its socializing influence, as believed necessary for the maintenance of our democratic ideals and institutions. To take the more gifted out of mixed classes would be to hamper the social develop- ment of students along the whole range of intellectual ability. Finally, differentiated groups would result in the isolation of groups, the end of inter-group understanding, and a diminution of a feeling of mutual respect for the other elements in society.[15] This view has not disap- peared even as we approach the end of the 1960's. There is now the additional factor of the newly awakened social conscience with respect to economic and racial integration. If the trend to homogeneous group- ing reverses itself in this decade, the reason will be essentially social rather than educational.

Most high school classroom teachers would probably agree that homogeneous grouping allows them to focus given lessons so that all of the students can learn and profit—to achieve the purpose, that is, for which schools were established. In a heterogeneous class, the most logical solution seems to be to focus on the average student in the group; the obvious result, however, is the loss of pupils at both ends of the intelligence scale. An impossible alternative is for the teacher to construct three or more separate curricula for one heterogeneous group. Having to do this for five classes per day would be likely to drive even the most dedicated teacher into industry. Homogeneous grouping, as a result, seems the fairest method for both the teacher and student. While each class is unavoidably somewhat heterogeneous, the range would allow the teacher a better opportunity to put his lesson on a level that almost all students could profit from maximally.

Recently, the time-honored argument, that the classroom is histori- cally an extension of the common school and should allow for a com- mon educational experience for all students, has been extended to the

tion and the National Council for the Social Studies (New York: The Mac- millan Company, 1944), Ch. III.

[15] James B. Conant, *The American High School Today* (New York: McGraw-Hill, 1959), p. 75.

point where homogeneous grouping is considered responsible for *de facto* segregation. Some studies also purport to show that the learning of the brighter students is not enhanced by homogeneous grouping. The classes that were the subject of these comparative studies, however, were conducted by one instructor who assigned materials to students of like ability in both tracked and untracked classes. The results showed no significant differences in the learning of the two groups. Not taken into consideration in these studies was the unused opportunity to differentiate practices and materials with tracked classes. The experience in the honors program to be described would lead one to believe that homogeneous groupings are valuable for both the advanced and lower levels.

GROWING CONCERN WITH THE GIFTED

The research division of the National Education Association in 1941 identified four school practices reportedly followed by hundreds of schools throughout the country in meeting needs of superior students: acceleration, ability grouping and enrichment classes, differentiated curricula and course offerings, and extracurricular provisions.[16] The various methods of organizing the education of the superior student, whoever it is understood he may be, have not proved adequate. Acceleration can be attained by skipping elementary grade levels or, in secondary schools, by either carrying extra subjects or going more quickly through the regular subjects. Differentiated curricula and course offerings add certain electives which can be taken in addition to the normal program of all students, or different curricula may be chosen by those with different goals. Extracurricular provisions for the more able student can include everything from a French club to a chess club. As for ability grouping and enrichment courses, in 1941 approximately 22 percent of the more than 500 comprehensive senior high schools polled had separate classes for superior students in the social studies.

The development of the Advanced Placement program by the College Entrance Examination Board has made provision for superior students. The program enables the high school student to take a college-level

---

[16] National Education Association, Research Division, "High School Methods with Superior Students," *Research Bulletin 19:* 156–97; No. 4, 1941.

The N. E. A., in its questionnaire, defined the superior student as one "distinctly above the average in general mental ability, in a specific attitude or both," with the term "average" defined to include those in the middle range of academic ability or aptitude found in all high schools and not simply in one particular school. The term "superior" was used, as elsewhere by educators, interchangeably with the Leta Hollingworth term "intellectually gifted" and with "high ability." There are many such terms and as many or more definitions of the terms. Whether a student is "gifted" at an IQ rating of 120, 130, 140, or 170 is an argument for the theoreticians.

course for which he may be granted advanced credit upon matriculation in college.[17]

THE NATURE OF ADVANCED HISTORY

Development of an American history course appropriate to the abilities and needs of able students requires principles that differentiate elementary from advanced history. The most comprehensive treatment of this subject appears in Chapter IV of Henry Johnson's *Teaching of History*. Johnson, drawing to some extent on Charles Seignobos,[18] describes advanced history as "thought about human experience." History concerns relationships, generalizations, abstractions, and thus ranges into the realm of ideas. Along with these considerations goes the understanding and application of historical method and the concomitant skills of investigation. Johnson's view of advanced history is accepted by Ernest Horn[19] and is alluded to by Edgar B. Wesley and Stanley P. Wronski.[20] The question appears to be totally neglected in other methods books.

Except for Mary Sheldon Barnes's method and the source publications and problems organizations that appeared more than half a century ago, teachers until recently had little access to resources for implementing Johnson's ideas. As if in answer to the needs of honors and Advanced Placement courses, the paperback revolution has opened possibilities for appropriate programs.

THE NATURE OF THE PRESENT HONORS COURSE

The honors program described in Chapters Two to Six was built on Johnson's analysis. Taking account of the high ability and achievement of the students and of their previous exposure to two cycles of narrative American history, the collections of primary sources were substituted for the textbook as the basis for study and discussion. Documents and selections from the writings of leaders in American politics and thought carried the class into the realm of ideas. Analysis of the documents and source excerpts introduced the use of historical method.

Use of primary sources is not the only possible approach to an honors program that involves the structure of history, the realm of ideas, and challenge to good minds. It is, however, one such approach. The experience in the course indicates that it offers promise for honors and Advanced Placement programs elsewhere.

[17] College Entrance Examination Board, *Advanced Placement Program: Course Descriptions* (Princeton, N. J.: Educational Testing Service, 1960), p. 7.
[18] Charles Seignobos, *L'histoire dans l'enseignement secondaire: La conception nouvelle de l'histoire: La méthode* (Paris: Librairie Armand Colin, 1906). Unpublished translation by Paul Lutz.
[19] Ernest Horn, *Methods of Instruction in the Social Studies* (New York: Charles Scribner's Sons, 1937), p. 139.
[20] Edgar B. Wesley and Stanley P. Wronski, *Teaching Social Studies in High Schools* (Boston: D. C. Heath & Co., 1958), p. 132.

Two: The Establishment of the Honors Program in American History

This program was instituted in a suburban community, located less than twenty-five miles from the heart of Manhattan, having a population of almost 80 thousand according to the 1960 census. The community's public educational facilities in 1968 included more than ten elementary schools, two junior high schools, and one three-year senior high school. About 12,000 students were enrolled in the public schools, of whom more than 2,900 were at the senior high school. Some 5,000 other students attended the elementary and secondary parochial schools of the city.

PROVISION FOR DIFFERENCES IN STUDENT ABILITIES AND NEEDS

The students in this community derive from diverse economic backgrounds, some coming from rich families, who live, in many cases, in $100,000 homes, others from poor families, who live in cold-water flats. Some students drive their own automobiles to school, while others must use welfare money to pay their bus fare. The city is about 13 per cent Negro, a percentage reflected in the student body of all the secondary schools. In addition to Protestants, Catholics, and Jews, whites and Negroes, there are also in attendance Chinese, Japanese, West Indians, Latin Americans, Puerto Ricans, and newly arrived European immigrant children.

About 40 per cent of the student population continues from high school into four-year institutions around the country. Another 20 per cent attends some type of advanced vocational or technological institution following high school graduation. For approximately 40 per cent of all students, high school represents terminal formal education.

HIGH SCHOOL TERMINAL PROGRAMS IN SOCIAL STUDIES

The terminal group, more often than not, takes the "general" course of study, while the middle group of 20 per cent mentioned above follows some form of vocational training. All of these less academically able students take world history in the tenth grade and American history in the eleventh grade, except a few who take the latter course as seniors. Their courses are usually taught as watered-down college preparatory offerings, with textbooks that the students find very difficult to read. Recently, four teachers on the social studies faculty undertook the challenging task of writing new text materials and developing a new history curriculum which may prove more valuable to this portion of the high school population. In general, however, as elsewhere, the non-Regents or general student is a forgotten soul who is essentially serving time until graduation or until he reaches the legal age to drop out of school. While the vocational student has the same unfortunate experience with his academic subjects, there is some attempt in certain subject areas to "relate" the course work to his vocational interest and—hopefully—specialty. Also, this student works for a minimum of three class periods each day in a shop environment, to learn his vocation.

PROGRAMS IN HISTORY FOR COLLEGE-BOUND YOUTH

The college preparatory group proceeds along one of four tracks designated, from the highest-ability group to the lowest, CP–1 to CP–4. The student is not "block programmed" in one of these tracks, but the track assignments in English and social studies and those in mathematics and science are usually consistent. The CP–4 group exists only during the first semester of each academic year, after which it is ascertained whether an individual has both the ability and desire to successfully pursue a college preparatory program. Usually, only a few of these students pass the first term's work and are moved into an existing CP–3 class. The majority who fail remain with the same group, whose classification is changed to non-Regents for the second semester. The CP–4 group is a last try at a college preparatory curriculum for marginal students, and it is rare that more than five of the average class of twenty-five qualify for transfer to CP level work at the conclusion of the first term.

The CP–1 group supposedly includes the most able students in the school. It is from the two or three CP–1 world history classes that the majority of the members of the American History honors class is chosen. Based on the Otis IQ scale of 140 as top, it can be stated generally that the CP–1 classification includes those students with scores of 140 to 128, while the CP–2 group roughly includes those students with IQ's of 128 to 115. The CP–3 group ranges in IQ from 115 down to the high 90's.

INADEQUATE OLDER PROGRAMS IN HISTORY FOR ABLE YOUTH

The methods used in the past to meet the needs of the high-ability students in social studies paralleled those of a majority of secondary schools. For years there was no attempt to identify the more able other

11

than to designate those who had signified a desire to attend college. Then, over a period of several years in the 1940's, in many schools homogeneous grouping became a recognized reality; by 1949 this high school had instituted its present tracking system. Even within this framework of grouping, however, the teaching assignment of the CP–1 classes was reserved for the teachers with seniority. For many years, then, the ablest students in history were assigned to two or three ladies of long experience in the department. The techniques employed by these teachers varied little from class to class, regardless of the comparative levels of ability. The courses centered around a textbook, and nightly homework consisted of answering "key" questions related to the six or seven pages of text assigned. One of these teachers had the students in her CP–1 class read aloud successive paragraphs from a review book. Occasionally a teacher required the students to consult two textbooks rather than one, and this was the extent of enrichment.

THE EMERGENCE OF HONORS PROGRAMS IN AMERICAN HISTORY

During the middle years of the 1950's, the complexion of the social studies department began to change. An influx of young male teachers brought new ideas and vigor to a traditional department. At the same time, a teacher with twenty years of experience in the department assumed its chairmanship and allowed free reign to the new appointees. The young men were well suited to teaching, had a good subject-matter background, and added a dynamic atmosphere to the social studies.[1]

AMERICAN THOUGHT CLUB

Realizing that the school was failing to meet the challenge of the superior student, a young teacher set out to reform the situation. To effect a full-scale academic revolution along these lines required the concerted efforts of the Board of Education, school departments, civic leaders, and parents. To look primarily to the teacher for profound reforms ordinarily would be like asking a satrap to set policy for a Shah. However, he established an intellectual extracurricular activity called the American Thought Club, to avoid the pitfalls of the classroom, and relied on voluntary participation of students outside of the regular school hours. Due to a double session schedule, the juniors and seniors were in regular classes from 7:45 A.M. to 12:19 P.M. and then had the

[1] Among these new teachers were Robert Doherty, presently a professor at Cornell University; Richard Whittemore, now a professor at Columbia's University's Teachers College; Joseph Katz, a former research assistant of Richard Hofstadter and presently a teacher of history at Roslyn (N. Y.) High School; and Raymond A. Ducharme, now an assistant professor at Teachers College, Columbia University.

afternoon free to participate in extracurricular pursuits. Yet, the activity adopted many features of a required course. Students had to meet definite standards of work quantitatively and qualitatively in order to remain in the group, and the only reward was personal satisfaction. The assignments dealt, through paperback readings and written papers that applied historiçal method, with such topics as the American Negro, social thought, and Social Darwinism. When a second teacher took over operation of the club in its third year, the senior group was so large that he found it necessary to withhold announcement of the room where the weekly meeting would be held so that only the most interested students would have the patience to search out the meeting place.

AN HONORS COURSE IN GENERAL AMERICAN HISTORY

When this writer took over sponsorship of the activity in its fourth year, the orientation had been changed from that which was wholly within the area of social thought to one which included more political, economic, and social topics. Units of work such as the effects of immigration, F. J. Turner's frontier theses, and the effect of wars on American history were included. Applicants for membership in the club were invited from among the students in the junior and senior classes. The selection of members became a serious screening process. First, the student had to volunteer for the program, thus giving evidence of intention to satisfy the heavy work requirements. In addition, the prospective group member needed high scores in IQ and reading tests as well as a fine achievement record in previous courses in social studies. Recommendations by past teachers were welcomed. Consideration was also given to those students who expressed a sincere personal motivation to participate even though their test scores and past achievements might be somewhat below those of other applicants. Twenty-one students were finally selected. A year later the school administration scheduled the club program as an honors course for seniors.

A SOCIAL STUDIES LABORATORY AND SPECIAL BOOK COLLECTION

Honors courses require library resources and should have work space ordinarily not provided for conventional high school teaching of history. During this year of working with the extracurricular group, the writer had accepted an instructorship in the Teaching of Social Studies at Teachers College, Columbia University. At the same time, a building program was undertaken at the high school that included the addition of three new wings and the renovation of the old building. Through the social studies department chairman, the writer submitted to the Superintendent of Schools a sketch of a proposed social studies laboratory and a request to include such a facility somewhere in the new school plant. After several conferences with the Superintendent and Head of

13

Buildings and Grounds, it was agreed to convert a proposed storage area into a seminar-type room for the use of the social studies department. The room would be located adjacent to the new school library, and its walls would be lined with bookcases equipped with locks. The room would have a movable partition so that it could be divided into separate work areas in which there would be several round tables and a long four-section type of table used for seminars.

The next immediate problem was to obtain the funds necessary to stock the book shelves with multiple copies of primary source materials and outstanding monographs. First we put together a proposed bibliography and estimated the cost of multiple copies of our hoped-for seminar room library. Having taught in the community since early Depression days, the chairman had many contacts with leading citizens, and it was their pledges of more than two thousand dollars, gained in less than a month, that attest to her powers of persuasion and community influence. Along with some school appropriation and additional contributions from various sources, and the diverting of a portion of the department's annual textbook budget, we found ourselves in the possession of just under five thousand dollars to spend for our laboratory collection. It was at that time that the writer left the school system to assume the instructorship at Teachers College. Before leaving, however, he drew up a tentative course outline for an Advanced Placement class which he left with the chairman, since she planned to teach both the Advanced Placement and honors classes. What happened during the ensuing two years can only be based on hearsay. However, it seems that the bibliography, course of study, and seminar room environment proved quite effective since, of the fifteen students taking the Advanced Placement examination, the chairman reports that on the Advanced Placement scoring system (a descending scale from 5 to 1) twelve received grades of 5 and three students attained a grade of 4.

It was agreed that on the writer's return the following September the chairman would relinquish the American History honors class to him. In addition he taught an American History CP–2 class, an American History non-Regents section, a CP–3 World History group, and a Problems of American Democracy class.

The author wanted his honors class to have wide use of the social studies laboratory, but, as we shall see, this desire was not completely fulfilled. He conceived of the honors class as distinctly different from the CP–1 and other honors sections which had preceded it. As we have said, these earlier groups simply had a title under which they gathered the more able students, but their work was not appreciably different from that of other college preparatory groups. It was hoped that the honors program in American History would go further toward establishing suitable levels of instruction and learning in the high school for high-ability students.

14

THE THEORY OF ADVANCED HISTORY

The rationale for the honors course reflected Henry Johnson's principles mentioned above in Chapter I. The program included some of the elementary history that is basically narrative and descriptive, as needed to broaden the accumulated experience and knowledge of the students. But for the group of able high school youth the focus was on more advanced history—on thought-about human experience. Advanced history includes theory—economic theory, political theory, social theory—and principles of geography, of economics, and of the other social sciences. Advanced history deals also with the generalizations and interpretations of history. Able students should certainly have a chance to explore the realm of ideas and to know and to apply the processes of historical method. These students should also have the opportunity to develop skills appropriate to their ability in reading, writing, discussion, and independent study.

How better to test out this theory of advanced history than to let the students delve deeply into the words and actions of those who have made our history, study what others have said about these events, and analyze critically the motives of men and the causes of occurrences which constitute our past and present? Advanced history moves into investigation or research in sources. We had the able high school students, and we had at least the beginning of a good collection of primary source and interpretational materials. The course combined these ingredients into an honors program, paralleled by systematic evaluation of the excitement, intellectual motivation, and growth that it might generate.

Three: The Backgrounds and Records
of the Honors Students

The criteria usually applied in identifying able students in the social studies include facility in verbal and written expression, reading speed and comprehension, capacity for generalization and for perceiving relationships, ability both to understand and to formulate abstract concepts, capacity for and resourcefulness in independent work, logic, initiative, and originality.

SELECTION OF STUDENTS

The American History honors class for this year was made up of twenty-four students who were selected by the department chairman and the guidance officers on the basis of one or more sets of criteria. Taken into consideration were the various IQ and reading test scores. Each student's achievement in the social studies was considered, with special value placed on his performance in the World History course and Regents examination. Teacher recommendations usually weighed heavily, especially in the evaluation of members of the junior class. This was because the juniors were coming into American History directly from their World History classes. Another important criterion was the individual student's desire to do honors work in a particular subject-matter area. Each student, when informed of his nomination to do honors work, discussed its implications with his counselor. Few students turned down this opportunity. Rather, the chief problem in selection arose from the student's unsolicited effort, or more often the efforts of his parents, to obtain an honors class assignment with all its attendant status and prestige. There also has been a distinct increase in recent years of keen competition for high grades and test scores among the able youngsters from ambitious families obsessed with admission to status institutions.

Exceptions had been made occasionally in this school in applying the elements of selective evaluation listed above. Flexibility was necessary to keep "late bloomer" and able students who had been stifled and unstimulated from being left out of advanced secondary work after they had developed a belated love and ability for inquiry in a given area.

16

The mobility of the student was a reality to which the counselors responded with flexibility of classification.

Included in the profile of class members (Figure III–1) are the various data which haxe a bearing on their original selection for membership in the class and on their performance as members of the class.

IQ

The Otis Quick-Scoring Mental Ability Test—Gamma Form is one of the most widely used IQ tests in the nation's public schools. In the main, it tests verbal ability, although it yields a single over-all IQ score. This test was abandoned in favor of the Lorge-Thorndike, mainly because the latter takes into account in its scoring the difference between verbal and nonverbal abilities. This test tends to register a higher IQ than its predecessor.

ACHIEVEMENT TESTS

Most college-bound students in this school take the Scholastic Aptitude Test during their junior year, and many also take one, two, or three achievement tests, depending on the varying requirements of the schools to which they are applying. Some of the students in the honors class took the American history achievement test before finishing the course, and some others, who were juniors, took the test early in their senior year.

The National Merit Scholarship Corporation has given direct financial aid to more than ten thousand students and their colleges from its inception to the present. Computation of the scores on the various parts of their test—English usage, mathematics usage, social studies reading, natural sciences reading, and word usage—results in a selection score allocated to each participant. In each of the fifty states, the number of semifinalists totals somewhat less than 1 per cent of the graduating high school seniors in that state. As a result, it is possible for all the semifinalists in one state to be below the cutoff point established for semifinalists by another state. In New York, the cutoff point for the test taken by the group of juniors was 150; the following year, it was 149.

The New York State Board of Regents gives state-wide uniform examinations in all academic subjects required by New York State for the high school curriculum. In the social studies field, examinations are offered in World History, American History and World Backgrounds, American History—One Year, and American History—Two Years. Each school district has the option to choose which examination it wishes to administer. All college preparatory students in this school were required to take the World History examination at the immediate completion of that course, usually at the end of the tenth grade. Also required was the American History—One Year examination which is

17

given at the conclusion of the one-year study, at the end of either the eleventh or the twelfth grade. The State's purpose in making the Regents examination mandatory is to maintain a minimum standard in all the school districts across the state. However, there is a great flexibility among the school districts concerning which examinations are offered and which students take them.

FIGURE III-1.

A Profile of the Honors Class in American History

Rank in Class*	IQ**	History Regents		SAT		CEEB American History Achievement	National Merit Score
		World	Ameri- can I	Verbal	Math	ment	
1–10	135	98	97	697	753	699	150
	150/139	97	97	683	800	767	152
	135	88	90	669	694	—	132
	150/139	97	97	715	689	767	149
	133/137	95	95	701	649	—	145
11–50	150/140	98	97	695	730	780	153
	150/135	87	92	702	634	—	139
	132	93	95	670	609	698	—
	139/134	91	93	644	657	680	139
	150/133	94	96	698	698	739	150
51–100	138/139	98	97	657	643	763	139
	136/126	92	77	592	622	—	124
	150/137	85	96	664	707	694	151
	130	88	82	635	668	—	143
	130/143	87	89	683	643	707	150
	134	87	92	658	546	—	132
101–150	146/138	88	72	666	592	—	138
	133/122	95	94	651	515	737	125
	112	94	95	645	497	702	129
above 150	130/123	92	90	521	606	659	—
	138/134	89	65	612	543	—	113
	120	87	93	590	538	—	136
	126	95	94	556	663	680	116
	122/118	88	—	502	548	—	—

* Only students in the college preparatory course are ranked: 393 of 732 seniors and 425 of 789 juniors.

** Single scores are for the Otis, compound scores for the Lorge-Thorndike verbal and nonverbal.

CHARACTERISTICS OF THE CLASS

For some reason, while this honors class appeared to have some of the outstanding history students from the junior class, the records of the seniors were somewhat less impressive. The three students who ranked one, two, and three in that year's graduating class took American History during their senior year, but were assigned to a regular CP-1 class. This may have resulted from oversight on the part of the counseling staff or may have reflected the desire of these three students to avoid the rigors of honors work in this particular subject. By contrast, each of those who ranked in the first ten of the following class, all of whom took American History in their junior year, were members of the honors class.

Of the twenty-four students, twenty-three were native-born and the twenty-fourth was born in Canada. Two were Negro, and one was Oriental. There were sixteen of the Jewish faith, two Lutherans, one Episcopalian, one Catholic, one Greek Orthodox, one Presbyterian, and two with no religious affiliation. Three students had parents both of whom were naturalized citizens; four others had one parent who had been naturalized. The parents of the twenty-four students were all still living, and all but one were high school graduates. Among them, thirty-five held bachelor's degrees, six held master's degrees, two held law degrees, two held medical degrees, and one held a dental degree.

The members of the class together had twenty-four brothers and sisters, of whom twelve were older and had gone on to college. Six of the honors students were only children, and seven others were first-born.

Outside of class work, every member of the honors group participated in some extracurricular activity. The class included two student body presidents, two junior class secretaries in their respective years, a former sophomore class president, the student body treasurer, and the former treasurers of the sophomore and junior class. Included in the class were members of the varsity teams in baseball, tennis, and wrestling, as well as six band and orchestra members and six members of the school choir. Four students were on the school newspaper staff, and one on the yearbook staff. Sixteen were active in temple or church groups.

All of the foregoing information does little more than to identify this honors class as an able group. Some observations, however, can be made. It is interesting, taking into account charges that the city provided inferior education for its Negro population, that two of the twenty-four honors students were Negro. The fact that twenty-three of the students were native-born and that, of these, only three students were first-generation Americans might have some meaning, as might the fact that sixteen of the students were Jewish. The students came from well-educated parents who raised comparatively small families, and thirteen of the students were either first-born or only children.

The diversity of out-of-class activities indicates a well-rounded group. Numbered among the honors students were student leaders, athletes, musicians, and those interested in many nonacademic ventures. Most consistent were their interest and participation in the activities of the youth groups affiliated with their houses of worship.

These students knew that theirs was an honors class. On the first day of school, they were informed that the work would be somewhat different from what they were used to and that the reading would be both greater in amount and more varied than they had previously experienced. They were told further that their grades would be based on the quality of their work in the special course of study for the class and that no special consideration would be given simply because this was an honors group. It was explained that, while the fact would be noted on their high school transcripts that their American history course had been in an honors section, they could probably obtain higher grades in a regular CP–1 or CP–2 class while doing less work. They were advised to consider this information for a day; then if any student desired to transfer to a less arduous class he could do so with no comment or ill feeling. At the start of this talk, their faces were quite serious. As it progressed, the majority of students began to smile with anticipation. No one transferred. The honors class was assembled. The task then was to provide them with an honors course.

Four: The American History Honors Program

In the past, the curriculum for honors students in American History had been identical to that of every other track within a homogeneously grouped subject area. The only differences were the use of a college textbook, rather than the traditional book written expressly for high school students, and "harder tests" on factual information. The honors class thus had consisted of a highly able group of students without an honors program and without challenge to the intellectual power of the class.

NATURE AND SUBSTANCE OF THE HONORS COURSE

During this year, the American History honors course placed main emphasis on the students' abilities to analyze logically and evaluate critically. Main reliance for printed material shifted from the textbook to a series of primary source documents and readings. "Recitations" vanished; the amount of discussion and the use of written reactions and student interpretations increased. The results of the experiment proved rewarding and gratifying to both the teacher and the class.

CHOICE AMONG ALTERNATIVE HONORS PROGRAMS

At least four possibilities were open to the teacher in developing a program appropriate to the potential of the students. First, he could select a small number of major topics for study in depth, or the "post-holing" recommended by Charles Keller, former director of the Advanced Placement Program. Second, he could maintain the coverage characteristic of surveys, but introduce collections of primary sources as a substitute, in the main, for a textbook and stress the application of the critical procedures of historical method. Third, he could make use of the growing number of publications concerned with new interpretations of major developments in American history. Fourth, he could stress advanced skills, appropriate to high ability, in reading, writing,

21

discussion, and use of historical method and guide members of the class into independent study.

The writer chose, perhaps unwisely, to combine, in varying degrees, all the alternatives above—unwisely, because on reflection he has concluded that during the second semester he structured the assignments more than he would do another time. Not that the students complained about the amount of work given them, but less structure would have allowed for more individual ranging afield and more independent study.

COVERAGE

For able students especially, coverage is the most expendable of curricular traditions, but the writer submitted to departmental insistence on a full survey to protect the interests of students and the school in results of Regents and College Board examinations. "Depth" is a relative term. As the result of maintaining traditional coverage, the optimum depth for very able students was not attained, but the consideration of many topics nevertheless went much deeper than the traditional factual-survey presentation.

PRIMARY SOURCES

Where most other American history classes had their reading assignments primarily only in the adopted textbook, the honors students were required to read many of the primary sources from which the secondary works were derived. The bulk of these sources which were required reading came from the following collections: *Documents of American History,* edited by Henry S. Commager, sixth edition; *Sources of the American Republic,* by Marvin Meyers, Alexander Kern, and John G. Cawelti, two volumes; *Heritage of America,* by Henry S. Commager and Allan Nevins; *Problems in American History,* by Richard Leopold and Arthur Link; and *Great Issues in American History,* by Richard Hofstadter, two volumes.

INTERPRETATIONS

In addition to the primary source readings, at the end of a number of broadly defined units of work the students were responsible for reading a series of essays written by historians and others representing differing interpretations concerning that portion of their work. These latter readings would either confirm or dispute the interpretation which had been offered either orally or in writing by the students themselves. This type of selection came mainly from *The American Past, Conflicting Interpretations of the Great Issues,* edited by Sidney Fine and Gerald S. Brown, two volumes; *Problems in American History,* by Richard Leopold and Arthur Link; and *American Political Tradition,* by Richard Hofstadter.

ADDITIONAL READING

The students were encouraged to read outside of the assigned selections. They responded willingly, but accomplished less than would have been possible if the required assignments had been fewer. Independent study was encouraged in this manner as well as through various written assignments to be discussed on later pages.

The course developed as one which, in scope, covered the full chronology of American history with certain selected topics about which the various units of study and groups of readings were centered. These topics included American Colonization, The American Revolution, The Confederation and the Constitution, Jacksonian America, The Civil War and Reconstruction, The Rise of Big Business, Progressivism, F. D. R. and the New Deal, and American Foreign Policy. The periods between the topics, as they developed, were covered by the student on his own from the narrative of the textbook.

THE TEXTBOOK AND ITS FUNCTION

During the first week of school each student received a copy of the textbook to be used for the course, *The Adventure of the American People,* by Henry F. Graff and John A. Krout. This was the only textbook with which they came in contact.

PROCEDURES IN THE HONORS COURSE

It was necessary, at the beginning of the school year in September, to break the students away slowly from their previous experiences in social studies classrooms. Although they were able students, they still felt great academic security in being given a certain number of assigned textbook pages to master and to know, through detailed subject-matter outlining in class, exactly what was expected of them. After about two weeks, we were away from the assignment of a set number of pages each night and had block assignments to be completed, ordinarily, at the end of a given week. After about two or three more weeks we had reached an understanding that the textbook was to be read to provide a factual background for the other assigned readings that had been made beginning in the second week of the term. All but a few students accepted this responsibility easily and well. Several stated their insecurity about this type of assignment; one or two could not be weaned from past habit and did poor work throughout the year. On the whole, however, the transition was smooth and orderly.

SOURCE BOOKS

Some of the selected readings could be found in more than one of the source collections used. When this was true, the student was given the option of which to read, even though the excerpts occasionally differed somewhat. This was done because many of the students bought their own copies of some of the source books so as to avoid the unfortunate bottleneck at the school and to have them for the convenience of home study. The option, therefore, allowed them to utilize their own books more efficiently. At the end of the school year, the class as a group had purchased extensive personal libraries for themselves.

THE CLASSROOM, THE LABORATORY, THE SCHOOL LIBRARY, AND THEIR USE

The class, of twenty-four members, met regularly in a thirty-seat classroom. About once every two weeks, the group met in the social studies seminar room where the multiple copies of source readings were shelved; at most other times the room was pre-empted for use by nine Advanced Placement students. Part of the resulting problem was resolved by removing a number of copies of the books used by the honors class to a reserve shelf in the school library. Because they found themselves barred from using the social studies laboratory at convenient times during the school day, most members of the honors class found it necessary to return to school in the evenings and use the reserve shelves of the library, which was open four nights a week from seven to nine.

READING ASSIGNMENTS

The reading assignments were made in blocks of ten to twenty selections each, each with at least one focal point but some with as many as three or four. The students were given a date, usually about ten days after receiving the assignment, to be prepared for a class discussion on the readings.

Most of the collections of documents have an editor's introduction both before each group of readings and before each individual selection. Many students chose to read these editorial statements after reading the documents so that they could form their own opinions and evaluations first.

DISCUSSION

Each discussion on a block of readings was led by a different student and usually lasted for three or four class periods. The student leader posed to the group certain questions that were thought-provoking and required careful analysis and interpretation of the words of the individuals who have made our history. The teacher helped the student leader to plan the sessions, if asked to do so, and served as a source of information and corroboration as well as a guide to avoid digressions in discussion. Only once was it necessary for him to take over from a student leader whose scheduled discussion was too loosely organized.

The atmosphere provided by these discussions was electric in nature. In the main, they were exciting classes for students and teacher alike. The initiative continually shifted from discussion leader to the balance of the class and back again. One student who claimed to be an economic determinist attempted to turn every consideration and conclusion in that direction. He did this more to bait the class than to express a sincere belief. Another student never came to class without brief biographies of all the authors to be discussed that day. He would then attempt to prove the effect of the writer's environment on his words and actions. Still other students would attempt to disagree with whatever interpretation the leader would place on a selection for the fun of seeing how logical another view would seem. These were not frivolous disagreements, but as valid, or nearly so, as the original position taken. One student, on occasion, when he was backed into a corner on some point, let loose, in a very authoritative manner, a flood of fictitious figures and evidence to see if he could catch his colleagues napping on his lack of documentation.

The response of the class was excellent. They all showed growth in the skills of both leading and participating in discussions. Every student knew that he had to be well prepared on all the readings or face some embarrassment before the eyes of his peers, who were caught up in the spirit of friendly but dedicated competition.

WRITING ASSIGNMENTS AND RELATED SKILLS

Almost always, the selected readings presented varying views on any given issue. About once every week or ten days, either the students were required to turn in, prior to the class discussion, an evaluation, based on their over-all knowledge in a given area, of the positions taken in their readings, or they were asked to give their own interpretation of some aspect of the subject area backed up with logic, critical thinking, and documentation.

During the second semester, a longer paper was assigned. It concerned a problem to be solved by use of historical method. Some of the topics considered by the students were Andrew Jackson's veto of the Maysville Road Bill, the origin of the Know-Nothings, the racial attitudes of Andrew Johnson, and the origins of Jim Crowism.

A week of class time was spent instructing the students in the practices and procedures of such an undertaking. Form and format were thoroughly discussed, and the historical method was explained. The students were allowed to pick their own area of study with the approval of the writer. They were given eight weeks in which to complete the assignment. At the end of four weeks they were required to turn in their bibliographies, to make sure that procrastination was not a common practice and to allow the teacher to come in with some additional recommendations if any seemed appropriate. When submitted in final form, the papers were evaluated very carefully. Close attention was given to writing skills such as logical sequence and full development of ideas, clear presentation in paragraph form, the proper use and easy flow of words, and the student's documentation. The main aim in having the papers written was to check on the students' use of historical method.

The whole exercise was included among the high points of the students' experiences as reported in their year-end anonymously written evaluations.

ATTENTION TO CRITICAL METHOD

Throughout all the class activities of the school year, constant attention was given to critical method. Whether the moment called for reading, writing, or discussing, the students were continually urged to sharpen their critical abilities. As Morris R. Lewenstein defines them, these skills include the abilities to identify the central issues, to use language accurately and precisely, to recognize underlying assumptions, to evaluate evidence, and to draw warranted conclusions.[1]

As time went on this urging was unnecessary on the part of the teacher. The members of the class kept each other constantly reminded of any deficiencies in these areas. Any time a student offered his own interpretation, his position was challenged by at least one other member of the class, and he was held responsible for documenting his evidence and his conclusions. This ever-present prodding by one's peers may have resulted in the withdrawal from group activity on the part of one or two students, but the majority responded with an increasing glee to this exciting mental competition, in what was apparently a new experience for them.

EVALUATION OF INDIVIDUAL ACHIEVEMENT

The school year was divided into four marking periods, and there were two uniform examinations: the midterm given by the school and the final Regents examination required by New York State. Many history classes at the school had almost daily quizzes, with a full-period examination at least once every ten days to two weeks.

PROBLEMS OF GRADING HONORS GROUPS

The question of how honors groups should be graded has arisen in many school systems. The manner in which this problem is solved varies from school to school. Albert F. Merz, Jr., the assistant principal of Nyack (N.Y.) High School, made a survey of selected school systems

[1] Morris R. Lewenstein, *Teaching Social Studies in Junior and Senior High Schools* (Chicago: Rand McNally, 1963), p. 386.

in New York State in 1960–1961. Of the 65 schools that he contacted, 57 offered honors courses. He found that 22 of these schools weighted honors grades in some manner, either by multiplying them by a certain factor or by simply adding a specific number of points to the honors grade. In addition, Merz found that most of the schools identified grades in honors courses on the students' permanent record card and college transcript.[2] Two years earlier, the New York State Association of College Admissions Deans and Guidance Personnel found in a poll of 113 schools that 102 made no provision for special marks such as those for honors students.[3]

The fear raised by most students and parents concerns the possibility of being hurt in one's over-all grade average and therefore in college admissions. A study made in West Hempstead, New York, in 1961 showed that grades tended to be the same regardless of group classification and that some students actually received lower grades in lower academic programs.[4] The conclusion was drawn that honors work does not penalize the student, and it was emphasized that student attitude is as important as the course and the teacher. The writer concurs.

EVALUATING AND GRADING THE HONORS CLASS

The students were evaluated on the basis of their performance as both discussion leader and participant and on the results of their written submissions, taking into consideration individual improvement as the term progressed. Formal tests and written examinations in class time were held to a minimum. In the American History honors class, two examinations during each nine- or ten-week marking period were the maximum. Objective-type short-answer questions were used only once during the year on one of the earliest tests, chiefly to bridge the gap from the student's previous social studies experience. Most often, the written examination consisted of one essay question to be answered during the forty-five-minute class period. The question, stated in rather general terms, allowed the student to take a point of view or one of many possible approaches and required him to back up his position with both detailed facts and documentation from the readings.

In grading, no floor was placed by the school administration on honors grades, and the instructor was not interested in coming out with a curve that could be used to demonstrate either the excellence of his instruction or his command of evaluation instruments. The evaluation here was necessarily subjective, but, one hopes, fair and equitable. The grading

[2] R. P. Brimm, "Thorny Problem—How Weight Student Marks in Honors Courses," *National Association of Secondary School Principals Bulletin,* Vol. XLV (April 1961), pp. 43–48.

[3] *Ibid.*

[4] "Does an Honors Course Penalize a Student?," *School Management,* Vol. V (March 1961), pp. 28–30.

scale was by number grades. It would seem very difficult to differentiate between a grade of 92 and 93 or 77 and 78, and so it was; but an attempt was made to assess each student's performance and comply with school grading policy. All members of the class could receive grades in the high 90's, or they could all fail, either extreme indicating certain conclusions too obvious to mention.

At the end of the first marking period, there were ten grades in the 90's and fourteen in the 80's. The grades for the second marking period again included ten in the 90's but then broke down to eleven in the 80's and three in the 70's. With twenty-three students in the second semester, the third marking period found fourteen grades in the 90's, eight in the 80's, and one in the 70's. In the last marking period, there were thirteen in the 90's, eight in the 80's, one in the 70's, and one in the 60's. These grades represented the teacher's evaluation of the students and were separate from their scores on the Regents examination in American history. These results tend to show that a majority of the class were up to the demands of the work and attained virtually the same grades that they would have received in a less demanding situation. There was a year-long consistency of grades, with only two or three students who could not or did not wish to keep up with the work. Interestingly enough, the student who received the mark in the 60's also received a 68 on the Regents examination, and the instructor had recommended that he drop out of the honors group at midyear because it was then apparent that his attitude was poor and he was not profiting from the program.

The grading standards and procedures applied by the writer to the honors class were the same as for his other college preparatory classes. The level of expectation was higher for the honors students, but the grading procedures were the same.

Five: Evaluation of the Honors Course

Not enough time has elapsed at the time of this writing to gain a thorough perspective on the course. College records are not yet available for students who were seniors; the juniors have not yet graduated from high school. The program of that year has not been repeated with other classes. What can be done, however, is to study those achievement records that are available and to consider any apparent changes in student attitudes and behavior which might be attributable to some aspect of the course. The self-evaluations made by the students can also be considered along with reactions within the school and among the adult population of the community. In planning for such an evaluation, the writer compiled relevant achievement records of the students, asked them to submit their own unsigned evaluations of the course both at midyear and in June, kept an anecdotal record of happenings during the course of the school year, and participated in many discussions with colleagues and townspeople.

THE INSTRUCTOR'S EVALUATION

The writer, in his several years of experience with other students, never had less difficulty in motivating pupils. The excitement that engulfed the honors classroom daily, almost without exception, was apparently felt by every member. A teacher with any experience knows that each class of students takes on a personality of its own. This honors class operated as a group with an attitude of co-operation and friendly competition. The group, with the exception of one or two students, was self-motivated and possessed a high level of morale. Interest in the subject matter continually grew, and many individuals worked beyond the scope of the assignments. This is borne out by the number of books purchased by the students for their own libraries, as mentioned in the preceding chapter. Another factor was their willingness to return to the school library several evenings a week. The only students who did not use the extended library hours were those few who had purchased a copy of every book used for the course. Even they would appear during the evenings preceding the submission of a written assignment. It was necessary to issue to one student duplicates of all school materials so that he could keep one set at home and one at school in order to overcome the handicap of extreme absenteeism due to ill-health. The previous year, this individual had been absent 85 of the 173 days school was in session. During the year in which he was enrolled in the American History honors course, he was absent from school during all or part of six days, but managed to attend the honors class on four of those days. This is an extreme example of the unusually good attendance record of the class members. Many students, although indisposed enough to be officially absent from school on a given day, still found it within their power to come to the school building for the meeting of the honors class.

USE OF PRIMARY SOURCES

The whole idea of approaching the study of history through the basic data of the historian—that is, the primary sources—was an unqualified success. In this year all students read the same selections, a procedure that was economical in demands on books and that simplified assignments and reduced confusion in discussions. Further development of the program might include some variations in the selection of readings and their grouping. In another year, with very able youngsters, the writer would include fewer required selections and many more optional ones to allow for more individual exploration of available materials. Coverage could be sacrificed for even greater depth and diversity of readings. Some, at least, of the students could also range further into differing interpretations of aspects of American history.

THE TEXTBOOK AND ITS FUNCTION

While the textbook can and should be de-emphasized to a great extent, a well-written, authoritative secondary volume can provide a needed service to the source-oriented history class. It can, when read as a subsidiary element of a course, provide the necessary frame of reference for the important work at hand. Too few juniors and seniors in senior high school retain much from even well-taught eighth-grade history courses. A running narrative can tie together the topics chosen for depth studies. The textbook can be given to able youngsters at the beginning of the year with instructions to use it as a reference volume. With such use the source readings can be placed in the whole perspective of history. Certainly, the textbook is the least important reading for the year, but it can provide a measure of security for the student.

SOURCE BOOKS

The main problem surrounding the use of source books was their availability. Ideally, each student should be assigned his own copy of each of the source books used. Without such a system there is an almost constant competition for the use of the volumes during convenient hours.

As for the quality of the source books used, the writer registers no complaint. Almost every week finds publication notices of new primary source collections coming out in paper. There is much overlap in selections, and one's choice would depend on the background of the editor and his rationale for his selection of readings to be included. Further opportunities for selection also come in the ever-increasing number of specialized collections of source readings. Two such publications are Eric L. McKitrick, *Slavery Defended: The Views of the Old South* (Englewood Cliffs, N.J.: Prentice-Hall, 1963), and David A. Shannon, *The Great Depression* (Englewood Cliffs, N. J.: Prentice-Hall, 1960).

THE CLASSROOM, THE LABORATORY, THE SCHOOL LIBRARY, AND THEIR USE

The honors class made the best use of the facilities available. A classroom was assigned to it only one period each day; the laboratory room, unfortunately, only occasionally. Lacking a workroom for the course, the members of the class worked on their assignments individually, for the most part, in the school library or at home.

The librarians provided excellent co-operation; as it turned out, they were willing to give about half of their time to the American History honors students immediately before and after school and from 80 to 90 per cent of their time during the library's evening hours. As a matter of fact, had it not been for their willingness to handle many copies of the source books on a reserved book basis, the course would not have been successful. At times librarians were issuing upwards of fifty volumes on an hourly sign-up schedule. This represented more books than they issued in this way for the other 128 faculty members combined.

An American history workroom or laboratory, preferably adjoining the library, would have saved time and work for both students and librarians. The class itself could have devised an equitable arrangement for overnight circulation of needed titles. In any case, it would seem to the writer that the loss of even fifty dollars' worth of books each year would be more than compensated for by the great increase in the use of these valuable volumes. A workroom would also have enabled the teacher and students to test the value of group rather than individual preparations.

READING ASSIGNMENTS AND RELATED SKILLS

The required readings, chronologically grouped and due about ten days apart, proved to be an efficient method of assignment. As we have said, it might have been interesting to have specified a topic or focal point and then let the individual student follow an independent reading program within the source materials. There is no question that as the year progressed, almost all students were more able to dissect simple selections, read between the lines, and relate one reading or group of readings to others of a similar nature. One student, for example, set out to "prove" that the length of a President's inaugural address was the

31

index to his "greatness." According to this boy's documented case, the shorter the inaugural address, the greater the President. Still another student drew rather a sophisticated comparison between John Adams and Woodrow Wilson in their attempts to keep the nation from war. It was startling how often the members of the class were able to recall the ideas of men studied months before, not only for details but also as a means of showing relationship or continuity.

DISCUSSION

Approximately four out of five periods were devoted to class discussion of the readings. On occasion the teacher used the class time to introduce a topic or set of readings or to summarize and pull together previous class sessions. There also was a day every two weeks or so when the laboratory was available and the students would spend time reading. It was in the exciting class discussions, however, that the students' abilities of critical analysis, logic, and persuasiveness were shown in their best light. The free-wheeling give and take, which wandered only occasionally and proceeded with a bare minimum of teacher direction or interference, was of the quality to belie the youthfulness of the participants. One should not neglect the self-confidence which grew in each student as well as his ability in speaking effectively.

WRITING ASSIGNMENTS AND RELATED SKILLS

The written work showed a marked improvement during the course of the program. This segment of the students' toil aided immeasurably in their understanding of historical method and affected their abilities in the field of oral discussion. Writing their ideas and being able to see in front of them the logical progression to the drawing of a conclusion, or in some cases the birth of an idea, had a visible effect on the quality of their thinking and therefore their over-all performance.

The writer would have preferred to have regular conferences with each student on his writing and his research procedures while working on the long second-semester assignment, but unfortunately there was not enough time available for such aid and criticism. Occasional conferences were held, however, with those students whose skills in these areas appeared to lag behind those of the rest of the group.

ATTENTION TO CRITICAL METHOD

As can easily be seen from the remarks on the writing and reading assignments and on discussion, there was constant improvement in the students' abilities to identify central issues, to use language accurately and precisely, to recognize underlying assumptions, to evaluate evidence, and to draw warranted conclusions.

One student argued midway through the year that the term "a very clever politician" did not necessarily have a bad connotation. According to him, a politician could not be classified automatically as a hypocrite, as he had thought some months earlier. Another student pondered with his colleagues how the course of history might have been different had Wilson been at Yalta and Franklin Roosevelt been at Versailles. There can be little question that such use of the mind is not found in the typical high school course in American History.

EVALUATION OF INDIVIDUAL ACHIEVEMENT

Uniform examinations, whether created in a single school or devised by the State of New York, are not intended for use with a group such as the honors class we have been describing. In most cases these examinations are administered to provide a minimum standard of achievement. Usually they are poorly constructed and deal with a good many minutiae, and quite often they provide for little discrimination on the upper end of the scale.

An honors class with a program such as has been described need not be concerned either with the minimum standard supplied by these tests or the fine details that they include. Advanced history is thought about human experience and gets into the realm of ideas. So, too, should the method of evaluation. Also these students were constantly being judged by both the teacher and their fellows. They were "up" every day. The writer would be satisfied and quite secure in his teaching obligations to do away with formal testing as we know it in the operation of an honors class like the one in question.

To conclude comments on evaluation: a teacher can enjoy his job only if he gets a certain return from his students, a satisfaction. This satisfaction can take many forms. Some college preparatory students express their gratitude and report the teacher to be marvelous because he helped them get a high grade on their Regents examination. General students manage to convey thanks in their own way to a teacher for having recognized them as individuals, for caring. The writer found, however, that the ultimate in teacher satisfaction comes from receiving the gratitude of a group of students for having helped them to learn—to master information, to work toward understandings, to learn how to learn.

SCORES ON SUBSEQUENT
STANDARDIZED TESTS

As we have seen in Chapter III, the students did well in both the American History Regents examination and the American History Achievement Test of the College Entrance Examination Board. The seniors who took the latter prior to the completion of the course did well, but not so well as the juniors who deferred the examination until the course was over.

One of the six seniors, who has since matriculated at Dartmouth College, was the only entering freshman to be exempted from both semesters of the first-year American history course on the basis of a competitive examination in the subject.

As can be seen by studying the class profile (Figure III–1), the honors students did not show any significant improvement on their Regents examination in American History over their World History scores. In any case, the class demonstrated that able students need not spend their time in memorizing facts in order to do well on Regents or College Board exams. Their excursion into sources and ideas may or may not have resulted in higher examination scores. It certainly incurred no penalties.

STUDENT RESPONSE

There was evidence of a significant growth in the students' interest in history.

INTEREST IN HISTORY

Foremost was the change of the students' minds during the course of the year's work concerning their probable college major field. Second, there was the number of books purchased by the students for their own personal libraries.

During the first week of school, the members of the honors class were asked to signify the subject field in which they thought they would probably major when they attended college. At that time four favored history. The remainder of the group listed a diverse range of fields including French, English, music, physics, pre-med, business administration, and political science. During the final week of school the students were again asked to signify their probable college major. Twelve students listed history as their choice. This group included three of the four who had originally made that choice and represented a wide range of achievement within the course. One youngster who had thought he wished to major in history prior to the commencement of the year's work had since decided on another subject for future pursuit. It is interesting to note that this one student received the lowest grades in the class both in the last marking period and in the Regents examination.

The American History honors class students took full advantage of the new availability of written ideas, as has been noted in Chapter III. It is evident that the publishing business has been revolutionized by the development and wide use of the paperback book. A great many more titles have been published at a more attractive price to the student pocketbook than ever before. It should be remembered, however, that the average family income of the students in this class was a good deal higher than the national average income. Although it was not done in this situation, book stores in most locations will give discounts to group orders on paperbacks, lowering the prices even further, at times by as much as 20 per cent.

Many times, as noted earlier, students who were reported absent from school for the day managed to be present for the fifth-period meeting. When full band or orchestra rehearsals were scheduled for fifth period, those members of the ensembles who were also in the honors class absolutly refused to attend the rehearsals.

STUDENT BEHAVIOR

During discussions with individual students, it was reported on several occasions that some of their fellow classmates were quite "different" in the American History class from what they appeared to be in their other classes. Some students' personalities seemed to change from quiet introverts to articulate participants in class discussion during meetings of this honors class. Some showed a sense of humor heretofore unknown to their classmates. These student reporters attributed much of this personality change to the atmosphere created by the individual teachers involved. To be certain, the teacher's personality has always played a significant role in the teaching process. While a student may identify his favorite subject with his favorite teacher, it is possible that this is a reflection of a form of idol worship; but for a student to decide to concentrate his study in a particular subject area, more is needed. In such a case, the subject matter stands alone on its own merits, and any human being who is interested in other human beings—what they do and say, how they think and react—is interested in the social sciences. It just so happens that history is the social science most taught in our secondary schools. The good history teacher brings in the other social science disciplines which are inextricably intertwined. The only necessity for the teacher is to kindle a live interest in high school history by accenting the meaning and value of human experience, past and present. This is not well done through the sole use of a textbook and the mimeographing of age-old outlines for student memorization.

During the critique session following the class test on the Civil War and its background, a statement of one student was noted which was quite typical of a very friendly hostility that was sometimes present. The essay question that they had been given the full class period to answer was, "What were the causes of the Civil War?" The lead-off statement directed to the teacher in a discussion of the essay question on the following day was, "Before, we could have answered that [question] easily, but now we know so much and have to think about so many things that it would take four hours to answer the question fully . . . and it is all your fault!"

STUDENT EVALUATIONS

The students were asked for an anonymously written evaluation of the course both in January and in June. The instructor felt that an open-ended question would provide a vehicle for the widest range of comment.

The main objection offered by the honors class when it was surveyed at midyear was that not enough readings were assigned. As a result, many readings not originally required were voluntarily discovered and assimilated into the students' knowledge during the first semester. This situation was not repeated in the second term, however. As the top honors students happily devoured the added amount of assignments at this time, scattered defections from consistent and successful work appeared among the junior members of the class. This seemed to break the traditional yearly student behavioral pattern known as "senior slump" since it was the six of them who, along with a majority of the group, approached the teacher twice to request additional vacation readings and discussion sessions. Apparently notification of admission to a college was not the usual beginning for a creeping apathy among these students.

The unsigned evaluations were overwhelmingly laudatory. All writers commented on how much more interesting the course was in comparison with the world history course which was centered around the adopted textbook. Most also referred to the fact that the current course was much more demanding of their time, to which the great majority did not object. Generally, they were struck with the difference of approach, with the extent to which they felt they were learning American history, and with the skills they felt they were developing.

REACTIONS IN HOMES AND THE COMMUNITY

Quite common were student reports of heated dining table conversation at home. As we have seen, a great majority of these students' parents were college graduates holding advanced degrees, and they regarded themselves as well-informed citizens. Several parents were allegedly reading the assignments along with their children so that they could argue with academic equality. One of the Negro parents was horrified at his daughter's critical appraisal of Abraham Lincoln and almost called her a liar, or perhaps a racial subversive, by stating emphatically that her information was wrong and her source more than questionable. The daughter rose to the occasion with her reply that her source was primary; "What about yours, Dad?" The father called the teacher the next day to ask where he could purchase copies of the books we were using, for he wanted to be able to argue intelligently with his sixteen-year-old daughter.

A handful of parents did complain, indirectly, about the amount of reading and questioned the value of working high school youngsters "that hard." "After all," the argument would go, "there is no reason to ruin their high school experience when college offers more than enough time for all that work." There were, in fact, two student "casualties." One of the honors students who withdrew at midyear suffered a form of nervous breakdown. Another student, we were told after the end of the school year, developed shingles which were only "partly" caused by his CP–2 American History class, the benevolent mother informed us. The great majority of parents were as excited as their children, however, about the program and tendered more dinner invitations to the teacher and his wife than he had received from all his classes in five previous teaching years. When it became generally known that the teacher was resigning his position at the end of the school year, a committee was even formed to dissuade him from leaving. This episode, the writer hopes, will illustrate the strong support by the community for the honors program in American history and the belief also that such a program required a dedication and enthusiasm which was manifest more in individual teachers than in administrative policy.

REACTIONS OF OTHER TEACHERS

The honors class was held during the fifth period in the school day, which was also one of the lunch periods. It was seldom that, on days when discussions of the readings were being held, there was not at least one other member of the social studies staff sitting in for observation. This started when one of the new young teachers asked to come in to see what happens in an honors class. She came back often, as did many of the other social studies teachers who had heard from her how informed the youngsters seemed to be. The students did not mind the visitors at all, and their presence may have even made their presentations more eloquent. Many of those teaching American history at school said that they were going to use many more source materials with their students. But they knew that their main problem was to gain access to needed publications.

TEST OF THE THEORY OF
ADVANCED HISTORY

Little doubt remains in the mind of the writer that Henry Johnson's theory of advanced history is a solid one. He is clear in the differentiation between elementary and advanced content. It appears, however, that elementary history, the narrative and descriptive, has value for able youngsters as surely as certain approaches to advanced history do for the less able.

There is, however, an important aspect of achievement which might interest the reader at this point in our report. This is the fact that the honors course teacher also taught, among his five daily classes, another college preparatory American history section of more "average" students, a CP–2 group. As an experiment, halfway through the first semester the CP–2 class was given about one-half of the outside reading assignments which had been assigned to the honors group. During the second semester they were assigned all the primary source readings given to the honors class, but were not asked to read the interpretational essays from *The American Past*. So far as achievement was concerned, the CP–2 examination quality rose steadily. On a Regents examination, most experienced teachers can readily identify honors or top group papers. About one-third of the final examinations written by the CP–2 students were indistinguishable from the honors class, with the exception of the two or three top honors students. When compared with the papers of other CP–2 students in the school, they were outstanding. The essay answers provided much more information and exhibited a greater amount of insight and deep understanding. These students had not merely memorized a set of outlines but read the actual words of those who had made our country's history, and this approach had profoundly motivated them to learn.

While all but two or three of the honors students appeared thoroughly to enjoy their work, only about one-half of the CP–2 pupils exhibited extreme enthusiasm over their extra reading assignments. The other half rather apparently did not care for the additional work for two reasons. First, some insisted that they could not understand many of the documents without laborious and time-consuming effort, and, second, some felt put out at being required to do so much more work than their group peers in other classes. The half that enjoyed the readings, however, did so with all the gusto of the honors group.

While the results of this instruction, as far as academic achievement was concerned, seemed to be significant, there were a few pupils whose response to the work was less than gratifying. In the main, however, the class not only enjoyed but also benefited from this scholastic experience. An example of this is the fact that all nine of the CP–2 students who took the American History Achievement Test of the College Entrance Examination Board scored higher than they did on the verbal part of the Scholastic Aptitude Test; six scored more than 100 points higher.

There are many possible reasons for the success of the source-reading approach to the teaching of American history. One cannot discount the element of novelty. This was the first experience of this sort for these students. Most new methods or approaches are greeted enthusiastically by students who feel excited at being a part of an experiment. There is little doubt that some inherent interest exists in the use of sources; certainly they offer more realism. Obvious, too, is the greater understanding which such reading affords. Another important possibility is the challenge of conflicts itself. This alone is very exciting to teen-agers, as is the opportunity to question, to interpret, and to conclude. When able youngsters encounter conflicting ideas, interpretations, and conclusions they can have a field day. This American History honors class did just that.

38

Six: Implications of the Study of the Honors Course

This honors teaching experience had a number of implications. Those drawn, however, reflect only work with twenty-four students in one class in one school in one community. Most agree with the conclusions of teachers in other school settings, but it must be remembered that we are dealing with but a single experience.

FOR TEACHERS

Teaching an honors class in any subject gives a kind of status on a high school faculty. To some, the assignment implies that the instructor is the "best" teacher in a department. This implication should most certainly not be the motivating factor for seeking such a class, if only to avoid arousing the petty jealousies often expressed in secondary school faculty rooms.

Other considerations, however, are more important in naming an honors course teacher. He must have a genuine desire to teach an honors section because he wants to associate with very bright students and wishes to enter into a co-operative study, in depth, of the subject matter. He must realize that many of the students with whom he will deal will be intrinsically more intelligent than he is, even though age and experience are on his side. He must be keenly aware that there is still much for him to learn, and he must be willing to do the work inherent in that learning. He must be a practitioner of historical method and have the ability to help his students sharpen their reading and writing skills even though they may have already made progress in these areas. In addition, the teacher of an honors class must understand the idiosyncrasies of very bright youngsters. He must be prepared to accept and encourage challenges of his statements, cope with brilliantly presented but faulty historical evidence, suffer with pedantic liberalism, and sympathize with the frustrating failure to capture the absolute truth about man and the universe.

TEACHER PREPARATION

Preparation for such a teaching assignment in history takes three forms. First, one must have had proper academic preparation prior to entering the teaching profession. He must have read widely in his subject area and have had the proper course work to ensure depth in his field. Second, in-service preparation is equally important, whether entered into through graduate courses or accomplished by independent work. Third, the teacher's own skills must be continually improved. Too many teachers stop learning when they gain tenure. Honors class teachers must continue to grow.

Daily preparation for an honors class is perhaps the most exacting task of all. One cannot "get by" with so much as a single day of haphazard planning. If there are twenty-four honors students, it is possible that several may not be fully prepared for the class; but the majority will be, so the teacher is always outnumbered. The students expect the teacher to be fully prepared; they deserve and demand his preparedness. If one does not meet their level of expectation and thereby loses their respect, there is no more torturing assignment in public education than this teacher–student confrontation.

TEACHING LOAD

It is impossible to deal properly with an honors class while also bearing the teaching responsibilities for four other classes. Administrative scheduling policy being what it is, however, this is the condition that most often prevails. It may have been possible to teach five classes every day of the working week when one preparation from one textbook was standard teaching practice for students of all levels of ability. With the significant change from heterogeneous to homogeneous student grouping, however, individual class preparations are necessary for effective teaching, and the dedicated teacher is stifled by the work load that his conscience and the situation dictate. Unfortunately, too many administrators and college professors either have never realized or have forgotten the extent of this commitment. For a teacher to be at the top of his form at every moment, today's scheduling must be reduced. Perhaps the most industrious instructor could handle four classes each day if it entailed a maximum of two separate subject or ability-level preparations, but a teacher of an honors class should have a further reduction to perhaps two additional classes requiring a single preparation. He needs more time for developmental work on skills and for scheduling individual conferences with students. Five classes a day with several different preparations mean no time for new and careful reading and no time for the stimulation of directed independent study on the part of the honors students. An administrator with the foresight to recognize the growing educational needs of our school-age youngsters would greatly facilitate academic progress in his school if he were to institute this more realistic, reduced schedule of instruction.

Such a move would increase expense, but so does the development of any natural resource, and the minds of our young people have been acknowledged to be one of our country's most vital forces. All fiscal problems in the educational sphere must therefore be solved, either through new sources of revenue or more inspired handling of educational funds. While this paper is not the place to deal with such problems, it seems necessary, if prosaic, to point out that a nation which is on the threshold of putting a man on the moon should be able to find a solution to such an important concern as the attainment of excellence in American education. The first step toward such an accomplishment is to change the public's preconceptions, and the educators' perceptions, of education from one of a static to one of a flexible form.

FOR ADMINISTRATORS

It seems that the administrator's part in an honors program is, first, to see to it that a valuable endeavor such as this is indeed instituted in his system and that the best-qualified teachers and students are involved. Second, he must appropriate necessary funds for the acquisition of materials and facilities to ensure the success of the program according to a predetermined set of clear and definite goals. And finally, he should be alert at all times to the possibilities of integrating such materials and facilities into other levels of the school body in order to utilize them most fully and effectively.

Teachers can desire change, but administrators, superintendents, principals, assistant principals, and quasi directors such as guidance counselors and department chairman must implement it. All of these are in a higher financial echelon than the classroom teacher, which perhaps implies that they bear more responsibilities, are more enlightened, and are therefore more serviceable to the educational establishment. Yet, ironically enough, they so often become preoccupied with peripheral aspects of education that they lose sight of the basic reason for the existence of our educational system and neglect classroom needs and innovations. It is at this point that the classroom teacher of imagination and energy assumes the duties of academic innovator or reformer in his effort to promulgate his ideas among administrative staff.

POLICY

It is necessary for each school district to decide on its own honors policy. The superintendent and the Board of Education have as one of their responsibilities to decide what they want an honors program to do and then to see to it that the principal has the necessary funds and facilities to make it successful.

41

The principal, in turn, also determines policies. The first, and most important, relates to the selection of teacher and students. The principal or department chairman who assigns a teacher to an honors class on the basis of seniority or in an effort to even out yearly schedules by alternating assignments is committing a grievous error. Yet this is done again and again. Some chairmen complicate policy because of a conviction that such a class goes along naturally with their position and that appointment of any other teacher to this class would impugn their supposed rank of "top" departmental instructor. Of course, many chairmen recognize maturely and candidly that their administrative duties are too extensive to allow for an honors class undertaking, or that their forte is more in the spirit of critic than creator.

Administrative policy also operates in defining the term "honors" and in determining which students qualify. Some principals take the view that the more "honors" students they can boast, the better is the school. Others regard all college preparatory youth as admissible to the special program. Either policy limits the matching of the requirements of a particular discipline to the interests and talents of a particular group of gifted students.

It is also important, for ranking students within the school and for consistent reports to college admissions officers, that administrators and teachers involved in an honors program establish, for the school as a whole, the policy in grading to be applied. Also important to some students is school policy concerning the Advanced Placement program. The graduates of a well-conceived, well-taught honors class could, most likely, do well with the Advanced Placement examination and be eligible for advanced standing in college.

GUIDANCE

The honors class was supposedly the top twenty to twenty-five students taking American history during a given academic year who met the criteria mentioned earlier. We have seen that this goal was missed for one reason or another, but at least the theory was honestly and clearly perceived. The successful selection of students requires the utmost co-operation between teachers and guidance counselors. There is no room for the so-called human frailties which might impel either teachers or counselors to push their pet students into the class or which might drive them to reject other faculty suggestions out of spite or malice.

EXPENDITURES

After ensuring proper procedures for selecting the teacher and students for an honors class, the administrator must turn his attention to the acquisition of materials and facilities. To be sure, this involves budgetary considerations which may conflict with the requests and needs of other programs which must be started or maintained. Yet it is the very art of administration to resolve conflict without forsaking a vital means of educational progress.

The writer maintains that students capable of honors work must be recognized and given the means to expand their capabilities and potentialities. To regard their intellectual restlessness, drives, and needs as self-motivating and self-satisfying is to deny the validity of institutional education and teacher excellence. Intellectual power requires stimulus and direction, which both materials and teachers must supply. Multiple copies of primary sources must be made available to enable students to work with and develop skills in historical method and steep themselves in the knowledge they crave. To have the students purchase their own materials is a subversion of a basic tenet of public education in most parts of the nation and is not often possible in less richly endowed communities. The solution of the financial problem found in this case is only one of many that are possible. The fact remains that some answer must be found.

From this experience and from the experience of other nearby schools, it can be estimated that the initial cost of reading materials to supply an honors class of twenty-five students satisfactorily would run in the neighborhood of three to four thousand dollars. It would then be necessary to supplement this book collection by books costing approximately an additional seven or eight hundred dollars annually.

It should be mentioned that primary source readings, which we are discussing for the honors classes' use, are highly effective teaching materials for lower-ability students as well if used with discretion and moderation. One must guard against the idea that only highly able and interested history students could benefit from use of sources. Our experience in this high school has shown excellent results from the use of such readings with college preparatory students below the honors level, and some teachers claim, from brief teaching experiments, that they are effective also with non-Regents pupils. Such selections in this particular experiment were taken from Richard C. Brown (ed.), *The Human Side of American History* (Boston: Ginn, 1962). Many similar publications are available.

FACILITIES

Also high on the administrator's priority list should be the provision of proper facilities for honors classes. Of extreme importance is an area where prolonged independent study can take place. An ideal arrangement would be something similar to the social studies laboratory, or seminar room, which was established here, even though the ultimate utility of the room in this particular case was not fully realized. Such a facility provides necessary materials in an atmosphere conducive to

43

work during periods longer than those which the arbitrary forty-five-minute bell punctuates for all academic efforts in our secondary schools. A proper facility can lend itself to the development of programs of independent study without interfering with the balance of regular school routine.

SCHEDULING

Thus another definite implication of our experience is the need for some flexibility of class scheduling. Why should all levels of American history need exactly forty-five minutes every day of the school week for forty weeks a year in order to cover an academic year's work? And if they did, forty-five could not also be the exact number of minutes required for the proper teaching of Latin II, plane geometry, physics, and senior English. Many school systems are introducing modified schedules that vary the length of periods from day to day and do not provide daily meetings for certain classes. Many administrators already recognize the need of both subject matter and brain matter for greater flexibility in class time. Psychologists tell teachers what has been evident to them for a long time, that attention spans vary from ability group to ability group.

FOR LIBRARIES AND LIBRARY POLICIES

The school librarians can be among the teacher's best friends. Usually they co-operate fully with teachers who do their part. But too few teachers ever take the time to see what library resources are available or to discuss student use of them. All too often, teachers send their students into the school library with some ill-defined assignment, not knowing whether there are sufficient materials on hand to serve the thirty to ninety students who will require them for the next day's work. A few minutes taken to discuss assignments with librarians can aid immeasurably in the efficiency and value of learning operations. The librarian will, in most cases, gladly give all the help possible in placing books on reserve and setting lending policies which facilitate a fair distribution of available materials. The librarian would also welcome teacher recommendations when filling her annual book order. Many times, she does not know enough about the various subject fields and their latest publications to spend appropriations to the best advantage. How valuable would be the personal requests or written bibliographical listings from faculty members familiar with the literature in their fields!

Regular library policies do not always lend themselves to honors work and the greater amount of independent study that such a curriculum should stimulate. In many schools, students may go to the library rather than report to a scheduled study hall. Taking attendance and accounting for books which students carry in and out of the library make a forty-five-minute study period wasteful of staff and student time. Other policies that limit the library's potential value include using it as a general study hall, using it for miscellaneous meetings during or at the end of the school day, and closing it for student use before and after school or during lunch periods.

The library in this case made a forward-looking innovation in its service during the school year in question, by opening the library for student use four evenings a week from seven to nine o'clock. Because it was a pilot program, records were kept of the number of students who used the opportunity, the courses and teachers involved, and the books asked for during these evenings. After an initial flurry of activity during the first two weeks, a pattern emerged that prevailed throughout the school year and to the end of the pilot program. The pattern revealed that 85 per cent of the students who took advantage of the service were members of the American History honors class.

The statistics suggest several possible conclusions. The writer may have been overworking his honors class. Other teachers and students may have been apathetic to the new library service. In truth, both speculations have some base. The honors students probably were assigned too much reading, but the impression is difficult to assess when complaints were negligible. Had the library possessed enough multiple copies of the source books for overnight circulation, or had the social studies seminar room and the school library been more available during the day, evening work except on term papers would have been unnecessary. It is also true, as in many schools, that both teachers and students were not taking full advantage of the library at any time of day. There are other school libraries which open during the evening and some which stay open for longer periods before and after school hours. In general, investment in multiple copies of needed titles rather than in overtime for libraries would appear to serve both economy and efficiency.

FOR TEACHER-TRAINING INSTITUTIONS

It would not seem inappropriate for teacher-preparing institutions to assume some responsibility for the development of honors programs in the secondary schools of their areas. In this regard, there are two services which could be rendered. First, these institutions could make a greater attempt to ensure that more of their graduates gain a subject-matter background with enough depth to qualify them for honors work. Second, they could make their students aware of the differences among the various ability groups and draw their attention to special methods and materials suitable for both extremes of the ability scale.

Another possibility could be a series of seminars or workshops in

45

which experienced teachers could co-operate in developing a type of honors course within the scope of their local needs and facilities. Special attention could be given to areas which have already been proposed by the Social Studies Department at Teachers College, Columbia, such as the distinctive characteristics of history programs for the gifted, the increasing number of resources available in paperbacks, and the skills in reading, writing, and investigation appropriate to high-ability students.

Encouragement should also be given to changes in the traditional textbook approaches used almost exclusively in American secondary school classrooms. A certain number of pages in the textbook each night, "key" questions to be written out as homework, and then a dictated outline on that material constitute the daily routine in too many classrooms with which we are familiar. This approach, considered either singly or in combination, is not intrinsically bad or ineffective if used occasionally as one of several patterns of teaching. As an exclusive format, however, it has proved to be dull and uninspired and highly ineffectual for both extremes of ability groupings.

There is also no reason to adhere rigidly to textbook teaching, now that we are witnessing a renaissance in the publication of primary source materials; the new publications are broad in their range and bound in paper or plastic covers. A careful perusal of bookstore collections would result in the discovery of readings appropriate, and very interesting, to all levels. After all, the dullness of many textbooks and of the usual nightly routine of "key question" homework seems to provide a block to student improvement both in skills and in enthusiasm. If, for a particular topic or unit, nothing is available that the student can read without considerable difficulty, the teacher could be encouraged to create his own reading materials, as many have already done. Time is needed for such a venture. It can be supplied either by a decreased class load or by paying teachers at their regular salary rates to work during the summer months.

One can easily see that, whether one bears responsibility for teaching the very bright or the very slow, time is needed to do the job properly. Therefore, to revert to a point made earlier, the teacher-preparing institutions could accept still another responsibility: advocating improvements in teaching conditions so that the level of excellence we all desire can be attained. There are very few teachers, if any, who can demonstrate creativity, imagination, and initiative in the classroom when burdened with five daily classes, a study hall of mob proportion, a homeroom which entails extensive clerical duties, and other assignments ranging from hall, cafeteria, or lavatory patrol to club sponsorship. Since the teacher-preparing institutions of our nation carry great weight both in maintaining present excellence and in fostering future improvement, they are not exempt from a certain amount of responsibility in challenging the conditions which impede top teaching performance.

FOR COLLEGE COURSES AND TEACHING

Implications emerge, too, from consideration of the effect of such courses as the American History honors class on college courses and teaching. For too many years, the colleges have looked down upon the high schools of this country, complaining about the poor preparation students receive prior to college training. Indeed, as late as July 23, 1963, the President's special scientific adviser, Dr. Jerome B. Wiesner, was still expressing these sentiments when he testified before the House Education Subcommittee. He stated that our colleges were more often remedial institutions than anything else.[1]

The colleges and Dr. Wiesner, however, have come to a conclusion which, while partly true, leaves one in doubt concerning their knowledge of the significant and growing exceptions to their generalization. Had they the time and inclination, they would discover many courses, in history and other fields, which antiquate a number of freshman and sophomore courses which they fail to condemn. The history course with which this paper is concerned is but one of the many which have been developed in public high schools. Students leaving these classrooms go to college only to be bitterly disappointed and bored by a repetition of high school material accompanied by inferior teaching. The results of this situation are either a loss of enthusiasm for college life or, worse, dropping out of college.

Some college professors who are aware of the growing honors work done in high school maintain that the advanced materials should be reserved for college use when student maturity would make them more understandable and meaningful. This attitude certainly appears to be without foundation when one notes that the students with whom they are commiserating get A's in their college survey courses without much effort.

Perhaps one way to clear the vision of many of these university and government people would be for them to visit the schools and actually see what is going on. Fine to observe would be the relationships developed between The Carnegie Institute of Technology and the Pittsburgh public schools; Teachers College, Columbia University, and the Roslyn, New York, public schools; Smith College and the Northampton public schools; and Harvard University and several of the school systems near Cambridge. The first-mentioned link was established by the exchange of college professors and high school teachers, with each going into the other's classroom for certain periods of time and learning from each other as a result. The second co-operative venture established an intern program which became an integral part of a large group–small group teaching organization of the senior year social studies classes.

[1] *New York Times,* July 24, 1963, p. 2.

Under this plan, Teachers College sends qualified graduate students out to work with the Roslyn High School teachers while the school board pays these interns approximately one-half of their beginning salary for a four-period day during the entire school year. Supervision is given these neophytes by both the high school and the college, and the program is under constant revision and examination. The Harvard intern program, employing a somewhat different approach, places master's degree candidates in various schools and turns over a complete teaching schedule for one semester or two, the salary being somewhat below the normal starting wage in that particular system. There are other such co-operative arrangements, one of the by-products of which is a fuller knowledge of each level by the other so that there can be steady improvement and reform on both sides of the educational division.

The existing college courses could be greatly bettered if two new attitudes were introduced to college instructors. One is that the method of teaching is significant in the learning process of even the brightest students. College professors all too often forget that the learning process involves more than the classic formula: bright mind plus interesting material equals inspired assimilation of knowledge. The ingredient which makes this formula a living reality is one warm, enthusiastic teacher. Unfortunately, this factor is more often subordinated to the needs of individual and private research insisted on by the colleges and universities. Class topics reflect the latest details which the teacher-researcher has uncovered, and the method of presentation is the lecture. Psychologists tell us that even the brightest students have relatively short attention spans; yet the psychology professors join their lecturing colleagues as they advise that lectures are not an effective method of transmitting learning. The social sciences particularly need a revision of college teaching techniques. The sciences offer, through their laboratory requirements, much individual attention that history and the social sciences, often taught in a lecture hall, do not usually provide. Motivating the students in this field, therefore, is a necessity; it can be greatly improved both by laboratory procedures in use of sources and by the construction of good and interesting class presentations. These presentations can include the reading, analyzing, and evaluating of source materials and interpretations.

In any teacher–student relationship on the high school or college level, a good deal of the responsibility for learning lies with the individual student. There is no guarantee that even the finest minds are self-motivated to discover and develop the values of such honors classes as the one reported in this study. After such a course, however, able students should be competent to carry on some independent study in high school and to enter college with power and confidence commensurate with their academic talents.

Appendix
Basic Reading, Required of All Students

In addition to use of a high school textbook provided to each student, Henry F. Graff and John A. Krout, *The Adventure of the American People* (Chicago: Rand McNally, 1960), all members of the class read Richard Hofstadter, *The American Political Tradition and the Men Who Made It* (New York: Vintage, 1957). They also read, ordinarily in chronological order, the following selections from primary and secondary sources in the six books cited, as listed either in their tables of contents or at the heads of the articles.

A. Henry S. Commager (ed.), DOCUMENTS OF AMERICAN HISTORY, 6th ed. (New York: Appleton-Century-Crofts, 1962)

Privileges and Prerogatives Granted to Columbus (April 30, 1492)

The Papal Bull *Inter Cartera* (Alexander VI) (May 4, 1493)

Charter to Sir Walter Ralegh (March 25, 1584)

First Charter of Virginia (April 10, 1606)

Second Charter of Virginia (May 23, 1609)

The Third Charter of Virginia (March 12, 1612)

The Mayflower Compact (November 11, 1620)

Fundamental Orders of Connecticut (January 14, 1639)

The New England Confederation (May 19, 1643)

The Navigation Act of 1660

The Navigation Act of 1696

Penn's Plan of Union (1697)

The Molasses Act (May 17, 1733)

The Albany Plan of Union (1754)

James Otis' Speech against the Writs of Assistance (February 24, 1761)

Objections to the Federal Constitution—Letters of Robert Yates and John Lansing to the Governor of New York (1787)

Washington's First Inaugural Address (April 30, 1789)

Virginia Resolutions on the Assumption of State Debts (December 16, 1790)

Hamilton's Opinion on the Constitutionality of the Bank (February 23, 1791)

Jefferson's Opinion on the Constitutionality of the Bank (February 15, 1791)

Chisholm v. Georgia—2 Dallas, 419 (1793)

Washington's Farewell Address (September 17, 1796)

Jefferson's First Inaugural Address (March 4, 1801)

Jefferson on the Importance of New Orleans—Letter to Robert R. Livingston (April 18, 1802)

Jefferson's Message on the Burr Conspiracy (January 22, 1807)

Madison's War Message (June 1, 1812)

Monroe's Veto of Cumberland Road Bill (May 4, 1822)

Jackson's Veto of Maysville Road Bill (May 27, 1830)

Worcester v. Georgia—6 Peters, 515 (1832)

Removal of Southern Indians to Indian Territory—Extract from Jackson's Seventh Annual Message to Congress (December 7, 1835)

Jackson's Proclamation to the People of South Carolina (December 10, 1832)

B. Marvin Meyers, Alexander Kern, and John G. Cawelti, SOURCES OF THE AMERICAN REPUBLIC (Chicago: Scott, Foresman, 1960), 2 vols.

Toil or Treasure: A Search for a Profitable Livelihood—from *Proceedings of the English Colony* (1612)

Powdered Wife: The Starving Time in Virginia—from John Smith, *General Historie of Virginia* (1624)

Pilgrims' Progress—from William Bradford, *Plimouth Plantation* (1609–1620)

We Conquer by a Drawn Game: Strategy of Space—from Thomas Paine, *The Crisis* (1777)

Winter of Despair: Valley Forge—from George Washington, Letter to Benjamin Harrison (December 23, 1777)

Speculation, Peculation, Idleness: The General's Despair—from George Washington, Letter to Benjamin Harrison (December 18, 1778)

The Completion of Independence—from George Washington, "Circular Letter to Governors" (June 8, 1783)

The Mad Cry of the Mob—from Abigail Adams, Letter to Thomas Jefferson (January 2, 1787)

A Little Rebellion Now and Then—from Thomas Jefferson, Letter to James Madison (January 30, 1787)

Northwest Ordinance of 1787

Benjamin Franklin on the Great Compromise—from James Madison, *Debates of the Constitutional Convention* (1787)

The Constitutional Convention—from Edmund S. Morgan, *The Birth of the Republic* (1956)

Faction: The Republican Disease—from James Madison, *The Federalist* (No. 10, 1787)

The Supreme Law of the Land—from Alexander Hamilton, *The Federalist* (No. 15, 1787)

Checks and Balances—from James Madison, *The Federalist* (No. 51, 1778)

Counter-Revolution: The Menace of the Constitution—from Patrick Henry, Speech in the Virginia Ratifying Convention (1788)

Inaugural Day in New York—from William Maclay, *Journal* (1789)

Republicanism Reviewed—from Thomas Jefferson, Second Inaugural Address (March 4, 1805)

Political Realities and Constitutional Scruples—from Thomas Jefferson, Letter to John Breckenridge (August 12, 1803)

The Menace of Western Expansion—from Samuel White, Speech in the U.S. Senate (November 2, 1803)

The Burr Conspiracy—from *Reports of the Trials of Aaron Burr* (1808)

Neutral Rights: Case for the Embargo—from William B. Giles, Speech in the U.S. Senate (November 24, 1808)

Old Republicans v. War Hawks: The Case Against War—from John Randolph, Speech in the U.S. House of Representatives (December 10, 1811)

The Nationalist's Reply—from John C. Calhoun, Speech in the U.S. House of Representatives (December 12, 1811)

Disunion: The Hartford Convention—from John Quincy Adams, "Reply to the Appeal of the Massachusetts Federalists" (1815)

Paradise Lost: From Agriculture to Manufacturing—from Thomas Jefferson, Letter to William Short (November 28, 1814)

Foreign Commerce—from David B. Warden, *A Statistical, Political, and Historical Account of the United States of North America* (1819)

The Missouri Compromise—from Hezekiah Niles, *Niles' Weekly Register* (December 23, 1820)

51

Two Worlds: The Monroe Doctrine—from James Monroe, Seventh Annual Message (December 2, 1823)

The New Adams—from John Quincy Adams, Inaugural Address (March 4, 1825)

The Benefits of Internal Improvements—from John Quincy Adams, First Annual Message (December 6, 1825)

Deism—from Thomas Paine, *The Age of Reason* (1793)

The Jeffersonian Republic—from Henry Adams, *History of the United States* (1889)

The People's Day: Inauguration, 1829—from Margaret Bayard Smith, *The First Forty Years of Washington Society* (1906)

The Regime of Democracy—from Alexis de Tocqueville, *Democracy in America* (1835)

The Democratic Career—from Alexis de Tocqueville, *Democracy in America* (1840)

Jackson Reviewing His Policies—from Andrew Jackson, *Farewell Address* (March 4, 1837)

Changing Views of Andrew Jackson—from Charles Grier Sellers, Jr., "Andrew Jackson Versus the Historians" (1958)

Manifest Destiny—from John L. O'Sullivan, "Annexation" (1845)

The President's Call for War—from James K. Polk, Message to Congress (May 11, 1846)

Whig Opposition to War—from Thomas Corwin, Speech in the U.S. Senate (February 11, 1847)

The Plantation as Big Business—from Federick Law Olmsted, *The Cotton Kingdom* (1861)

Masters and Poor Whites: Dissent from Within—from Hinton Rowan Helper, *The Impending Crisis of the South* (1857)

The Ethic of the Master Race—from George Fitzhugh, *Cannibals All! or, Slaves Without Masters* (1857)

Union in Balance: Sectional Logic—from John C. Calhoun, Speech in the U.S. Senate (March 4, 1850)

Union by Concession: Nationalist Logic—from Daniel Webster, Speech in the U.S. Senate (March 7, 1850)

To Each His Own—from Stephen A. Douglas, Opening Speech at Alton, Illinois (October 15, 1858)

Right or Wrong? A National Question—from Abraham Lincoln, Reply at Alton, Illinois (October 15, 1858)

For Georgia and the Union: A Plea for Prudence—from Alexander H. Stephens, Speech in the Georgia House of Representatives (November 14, 1860)

Not Enemies but Friends: Lincoln's First Inaugural—from Abraham Lincoln, First Inaugural Address (March 4, 1861)

Sumter Is Lost: The North Is United—from an Editorial, New York Tribune (April 7, 1861)

The Populist Revolt—from the Populist Party Platform (July 4, 1892)

Inflationism and Protectionism: A Plague on Both Your Houses—from E. L. Godkin, *Problems of Modern Democracy* (1896)

The Cross of Gold—from William Jennings Bryan, Speech in the Chicago Democratic Convention (July 8, 1896)

St. George and St. Vitus: The Personality of Theodore Roosevelt—from Mark Sullivan, *Our Times* (1930)

Nation and Corporation: The Square Deal—from Theodore Roosevelt, Fifth Annual Message (December 5, 1905)

Supreme Court Decision and Dissent: "Mere Size Is No Offense"—from *United States v. United States Steel Corporation* (1920)

The System of Bob La Follette: A Muckracker's Tale—from Lincoln Steffens, *The Struggle for Self-Government* (1906)

"The New Spirit": Piecemeal Revolution—from Walter E. Weyl, *The New Democracy* (1912)

Thunder on the Left: The Socialist Appeal—from Eugene V. Debs, Speech at the Indianapolis Socialist Party Convention (May ?, 1912)

The New Freedom—from Woodrow Wilson, First Inaugural Address (March 4, 1913)

The New Manifest Destiny—from Alfred T. Mahan, *The Problem of Asia* (1900)

Spanish Concessions: Moves to Avoid War—from Polo de Bernabé, Memorandum to John Sherman (April 10, 1898)

Humanity and the National Interest: Grounds for War—from William McKinley, Message to Congress (April 11, 1898)

Defense of Republican Policy: Our Duty in the Philippines—from Elihu Root, Address at Canton, Ohio (October 24, 1900)

Anti-Imperialism: The Power of American Example—from William Jennings Bryan, Speech at the Indianapolis Democratic Convention (August 8, 1900)

Independence with Strings: Cuban Remedy—from Elihu Root, Report of the Secretary of War (1901)

The Big Stick: Santa Domingo and Panama—from Theodore Roosevelt, *Autobiography* (1913)

The Convenient Revolution: Colombia's Protest over Panama—from Rafael Reyes, Message to John Hay (December 23, 1903)

The North American Peril—from F. García Calderón, *Latin America* (1913)

Triumphant Democracy: An Industrialist's Optimism—from Andrew Carnegie, *Triumphant Democracy* (1886)

Corruption and Decay: A Poet's Diagnosis—from Walt Whitman, *Democratic Vistas* (1871)

Progress and Poverty: A Reformer's Analysis—from Henry George, *Progress and Poverty* (1879)

Wealth and Morality: A Traditional View of the American Success Story—from Horatio Alger, *Fame and Fortune* (1868)

Conspicuous Waste and Pecuniary Emulation: A Social Scientist's Theory of the Leisure Class—from Thorstein Veblen, *The Theory of the Leisure Class* (1899)

The Social Gospel: A Re-evaluation of Religion in a Business Society— from Walter Rauschenbusch, *Christianizing the Social Order* (1913)

The Social Gospel in Action: Hull House—from Jane Addams, *Twenty Years at Hull House* (1910)

The Survival of the Unfittest: A "Scientific" Objection to Social Reform—from William Graham Summer, "The Challenge of Facts" (1914)

The Progressive Mentality—from George E. Mowry, *The Era of Theodore Roosevelt, 1900–1912* (1958)

Racism and Imperialism—from Richard Hofstadter, *Social Darwinism in American Thought* (1955)

Wilsonian Neutrality: The Role of the Peacemaker—from Woodrow Wilson, Appeal for Neutrality (August 19, 1914)

Submarine Warfare: The German Case—from Count von Bernstorff, Message to Robert Lansing (January 31, 1917)

Appeal to Arms—from Woodrow Wilson, Message to Congress (April 2, 1917)

Opposition to War—from George Norris, Speech in the U.S. Senate (April 4, 1917)

The Fourteen Points—from Woodrow Wilson, Address to Congress (January 8, 1918)

The League of Nations: Hope of the World—from Woodrow Wilson, Address to the U.S. Senate (July 10, 1919)

The League of Nations: Deformed Experiment—from Henry Cabot Lodge, Speech in the U.S. Senate (August 12, 1919)

Technology and Social Invention: The Cultural Lag—from the President's Research Committee on Social Trends, *Recent Social Trends* (1933)

Alcohol and Al Capone—from Frederick Lewis Allen, *Only Yesterday* (1931)

American and Un-American: For Restriction of Aliens—from Henry Pratt Fairchild, *The Melting-Pot Mistake* (1926)

Apple of Discord: The Dangers of a Discriminatory Immigration Law —from Louis Marshall, Letter to President Calvin Coolidge (May 22, 1924)

Anarchy and Sedition Laws: The Red Scare and the Courts—from *Gitlow* v. *New York* (1925)

Calvin Coolidge: The Business of America Is Business—from William Allen White, *Calvin Coolidge* (1925)

Al Smith: Up from City Streets—from Walter Lippmann, "Al Smith: A Man of Destiny" (December 1925)

Herbert Hoover: Prosperity Through Individualism—from Herbert Hoover, Speech at New York City (October 22, 1928)

Nothing to Fear But Fear Itself—from Franklin D. Roosevelt, First Inaugural Address (March 4, 1933)

Recovery: Economics of the Brain Trust—from Rexford Guy Tugwell, "The Economics of the Recovery Program" (November 16, 1933)

Recovery: A Critique of the New Deal—from The Brookings Institution, *The Recovery Problem in the United States* (1936)

Justice: Public Works and Social Security—from Franklin D. Roosevelt, Annual Message to Congress (January 4, 1935)

Share Our Wealth: Louisiana Hayride—from Huey Long, Letter to Members of the Share Our Wealth Society (May 23, 1935)

That Man—from John T. Flynn, *Country Squire in the White House* (1940)

As He Sees Himself: The Fighting Liberal—from Anne O'Hare McCormick, "As He Sees Himself" (October 16, 1938)

Wilson and the Great Debate—from Arthur S. Link, *Wilson the Diplomatist* (1957)

Conformity in the Twenties—from Oscar Handlin, *The American People in the Twentieth Century* (1954)

Roosevelt and the Middle Course—from Frank Freidel, *The New Deal in Historical Perspective* (1959)

Mirages and Realities of American Security—from Walter Lippmann, *U.S. Foreign Policy* (1943)

Two Worlds: Continental Americanism—from Charles A. Beard, *A Foreign Policy for America* (1940)

I Hate War—from Franklin D. Roosevelt, Radio Address (September 3, 1939)

Arsenal of Democracy—from Franklin D. Roosevelt, Radio Address (December 29, 1940)

Common Aims: The Atlantic Charter—from Franklin D. Roosevelt, Message to Congress (August 21, 1941)

America First: The Case for Isolation—from Charles A. Lindbergh, "A Letter to Americans" (1941)

Pearl Harbor: The Roosevelt Administration, Pro and Con—from U.S. Congress, *Investigation of the Pearl Harbor Attack* (1946)

Limited Victory: The Burden of the Past—from George F. Kennan, *American Diplomacy, 1900–1950* (1952)

The Spectre of the Bomb—from John Hersey, *Hiroshima* (1946)

The Iron Curtain: End of the Grand Alliance—from Winston Churchill, Speech at Fulton, Missouri (March 5, 1946)

Reconstruction: The Marshall Plan—from George C. Marshall, Address at Harvard University (June 5, 1947)

Containment and Point Four: Policies of the Truman Administration—from Harry S. Truman, Address at Little Rock, Arkansas (June 11, 1949)

Calculated Risk: Police Action in Korea—from Dean Acheson, Statement Before the U.S. Senate Committees on Foreign Relations and the Armed Services (June 1, 1951)

Failure by Default: Republican Critique—from Robert A. Taft, *A Foreign Policy for Americans* (1951)

The Fall of New Dealism and the McCarthy Reaction—from Eric F. Goldman, *The Crucial Decade* (1956)

The Supreme Court on School Desegregation—from *Brown* et al. v. *Board of Education of Topeka, Kan.*, et al. (May 17, 1954)

Constancy in a Changing World: The Permanence of Moral Law—from John Foster Dulles, "Challenge and Response in United States Policy" (1957)

Needed: A Sense of Purpose, a New Creative Policy—from Adlai E. Stevenson, "Putting First Things First" (1960)

The Lonely Crowd—from David Riesman, "The Saving Remnant: A Study of Character" (1960)

The Search for Southern Identity—from C. Vann Woodward, "The Search for Southern Identity" (1958)

Corporate Power and Democracy—from Adolf A. Berle, Jr., *The 20th Century Capitalist Revolution* (1954)

The New Face of American Labor—from Daniel Bell, "The Capitalism of the Proletariat?" (1958)

Science and Secrecy—from Edward Shils, "Security and Science Sacrificed to Loyalty" (1955)

Liberalism, Conservatism, Wisdom—from Irving Kristol, "Old Truths and the New Conservatism" (1958)

C. Henry S. Commager and Allan Nevins (eds.), THE HERITAGE OF AMERICA (Boston: Little, Brown, 1951)

Wouter Van Twiller Rules in New Amsterdam—by Washington Irving, A History of New York

The Puritans Hunt Witches in Salem—from Cotton Mather, The Wonders of the Invisible World

Nathaniel Bacon Rebels against Governor Berkeley—from The Virginia Rebellion in the Seventeenth Century, by T.M.

Sarah Knight Travels from Boston to New York—from The Journals of Madam Knight

German Redemptioners Take Ship to Pennsylvania—from Gottlieb Mittelberger's Journey to Pennsylvania in the Year 1750

Ethan Allen Captures Fort Ticonderoga—from Ethan Allen, Narrative of Captivity

Shaw Deplores Conditions in the American Army—from The Journals of Major Samuel Shaw

The American Army Suffers at Valley Forge—from The Chevalier de Pontgibaud, A French Volunteer of the War of Independence

Mutiny in the Pennsylvania Line—from The Journals of Major Samuel Shaw

The Bonhomme Richard Defeats the Serapis—from R. C. Sands, Life and Correspondence of John Paul Jones

The World Turned Upside Down at Yorktown—from James Thacher, Military Journal during the American Revolution

Major Pierce Limns the Fathers of the Constitution—from Notes of Major William Pierce in the Federal Convention

Washington Is Inaugurated President—from Elias Boudinot, Letter to His Wife

Jefferson and Hamilton Strike a Bargain—from Thomas Jefferson, The Anas

"This Government, the World's Best Hope"—from Thomas Jefferson, First Inaugural Address (1801)

John Marshall Expounds the Constitution

America, the Hope of the World—from David Ramsay, The History of the American Revolution

D. Richard Hofstadter (ed.), GREAT ISSUES IN AMERICAN HISTORY (New York: Vintage, 1959), 2 vols.

Andrew Jackson, Veto of Maysville Road Bill (May 27, 1830)

Henry Clay, Speech on the Maysville Road Veto (August 3, 1830)

Andrew Jackson, Proclamation to the People of South Carolina (December 10, 1832)

Andrew Jackson, Bank Veto Message (July 10, 1832)

Daniel Webster, Speech on Jackson's Veto of the United States Bank Bill (July 11, 1832)

Charles River Bridge v. *Warren Bridge* (1837)

Joseph Story, Dissenting Opinion in *Charles River Bridge* v. *Warren Bridge* (1837)

Lincoln Steffens, *The Shame of the Cities* (1904)

George Washington Plunkitt, Honest Graft (1905)

Walter Lippmann, "The Themes of Muckracking" (1914)

Lochner v. *New York* (1905)

Oliver Wendell Holmes, Dissenting Opinion in *Lochner* v. *New York* (1905)

Muller v. *Oregon* (1908)

David Wilcox, Testimony on Railroad Reform (January 21, 1905)

William P. Hepburn, Speech on Railroad Reform (February 7, 1906)

William Allen White, *The Old Order Changeth* (1910)

Elihu Root, Experiments in Government (1913)

Theodore Roosevelt, Acceptance Speech (August 6, 1912)

Woodrow Wilson, *The New Freedom* (1913)

Report of the Pujo Committee (February 28, 1913)

Woodrow Wilson, First Inaugural Address (March 4, 1913)

Josiah Strong, *Our Country* (1885)

Henry Cabot Lodge, "Our Blundering Foreign Policy" (March 1895)

Walter Hines Page, "The War with Spain and After" (June 1898)

Platform of the American Anti-Imperialist League (October 17, 1899)

E. Richard W. Leopold and Arthur S. Link (eds.), PROBLEMS IN AMERICAN HISTORY (Englewood Cliffs, N.J.: Prentice-Hall, 1953)

Carnegie, The Robber Baron (Matthew Josephson, 1934)

Carnegie and the Gospel of Wealth (Andrew Carnegie, 1889)

Rockefeller, The Farsighted Planner (Allan Nevins, 1940)

The Standard Oil, an Unscrupulous Monopoly (Henry D. Lloyd, 1894)

Collective Bargaining (John Mitchell, 1903)

Liberty or Unions? (James P. Boyd, 1894)

The New Immigration (United American Mechanics, 1910)

The Gates of Asylum (I. A. Hourwich, 1919; Woodrow Wilson, 1915)

White Supremacy (Alfred H. Stone, 1908)

Negro Ideals (W. E. B. Du Bois, 1903)

The Anti-Communist Raids (New York *Times,* January 4, 1920)

In Defense of the Raids (A. Mitchell Palmer, 1920)

For Social Advance (John Haynes Holmes, 1924)

For Individual Freedom (Clarence Darrow, 1924)

The Far Eastern Clauses (Department of State, February 11, 1946)

A Justification of the Yalta Agreements (Edward R. Stettinius, Jr., 1949)

The Betrayal of the Free World (John T. Flynn, 1951)

The Inevitable Tragedy (Dean G. Acheson, June 4, 1951)

The Obvious Treason (Joseph R. McCarthy, February 12, 1950)

The President Explains His Action (Harry S. Truman, June 27, 1950)

The President Should Have Consulted Congress (Robert A. Taft, June 28, 1950)

F. Sidney Fine and Gerald S. Brown (eds.), THE AMERICAN PAST (New York: Macmillan, 1961), 2 vols. 1957

Frederick B. Tolles, "The American Revolution Considered as a Social Movement: A Re-evaluation—from *American Historical Review*

Clarence L. Ver Steeg, "The American Revolution Considered as an Economic Movement"—from *Huntington Library Quarterly*

Charles A. Beard, "An Economic Interpretation of the Constitution of The United States"—from

Douglas Adair, "The Tenth Federalist Revisited"—from *William and Mary Quarterly*

Julius W. Pratt, "The Expansionists of 1812"—from *Expansionists of 1812*

A. L. Burt, "War of 1812: Causes, from 1809"—from *The United States, Great Britain, and British North America from the Revolution to the Establishment of Peace after the War of 1812*

U. B. Phillips, "Plantation Labor"—from *American Negro Slavery*

Kenneth M. Stampp, "The Historian and Southern Negro Slavery"— from *American Historical Review*

Bernard DeVoto, "Build Thee More Stately Mansions"—from *The Year of Decision: 1846*

Albert K. Weinberg, "Extension of the Area of Freedom"—from *Manifest Destiny: A Study of Nationalist Expansion in American History*

J. C. Randall, "The Blundering Generation"—from *Mississippi Valley Historical Review*

Pieter Geyl, "The American Civil War and the Problem of Inevitability"—from *Debates with Historians*

Chester McArthur Destler, "Entrepreneurial Leadership Among 'Robber Barons': A Trial Balance"—from *The Tasks of Economic History*

Thomas C. Cochran, "The Legend of the Robber Barons"—from *The Pennsylvania Magazine of History and Biography*

Henry Pratt Fairchild, "A New Menace"—from *The Melting-Pot Mistake*

Oscar Handlin, "What Happened to Race?"—from *Race and Nationality in American Life*

Robert E. Riegel, "Current Ideas of the Significance of the United States Frontier"—from *Revista de Historia de America*

Ray Allen Billington, "How the Frontier Shaped the American Character"—from *American Heritage*

Harry Elmer Barnes, "The United States and the First World War"—from *War in the Twentieth Century*

Arthur S. Link, "Wilson and American Neutrality, 1914–1917"—from *Wilson the Diplomatist*

Walter Johnson, "Senatorial Strategy, 1919–20 . . ."—from *The Antioch Review*

Thomas A. Bailey, "The Supreme Infanticide"—from *Woodrow Wilson and the Great Betrayal*

Eric F. Goldman, "The New Deal and Its Antecedents"—from *Rendezvous with Destiny*

Richard Hofstadter, "From Progressivism to the New Deal"—from *The Age of Reform*

Charles C. Tansill, "The United States Moves to War against Japan"—from *Perpetual War for Perpetual Peace* and *Back Door to War*

Herbert Feis, "War Came at Pearl Harbor: Suspicions Considered"—from *The Yale Review*

Godfrey P. Schmidt, "Senator McCarthy: A Martyr for Civil Liberties"—from *The Catholic World*

Richard H. Rovere, "McCarthyism in Retrospect"—from *The New Republic*

Merlo J. Pusey, "Measure of the Man"—from *Eisenhower the President*

William V. Shannon, "Eisenhower as President: A Critical Appraisal of the Record"—from *Commentary*

Bibliography
THE DEVELOPMENT OF
HIGH SCHOOL HISTORY

American Historical Association. *Conclusions and Recommendations of the Commission,* Report of the Commission on the Social Studies, Part XVI. New York: Scribner, 1934.

―――. *The Study of History in Schools,* Report to the American Historical Association by the Committee of Seven. New York: Macmillan, 1899.

―――. *The Study of History in Secondary Schools,* Report to the American Historical Association by a Committee of Five. New York: Macmillan, 1911.

BEARD, CHARLES A. *A Charter for the Social Sciences in the Schools,* Report of the Commission on the Social Studies, Part I. New York: Scribner, 1932.

CONANT, JAMES B. *The American High School Today.* New York: McGraw-Hill, 1959.

HENDRICKS, LUTHER V. *James Harvey Robinson, Teacher of History.* New York: King's Crown Press, 1946.

HORN, ERNEST. *Methods of Instruction in the Social Studies,* Report of the Commission on the Social Studies, Part XIII. New York: Scribner, 1937.

HUNT, ERLING M. "More American History?," *Social Education,* Vol. VI (October 1942), pp. 250–252.

―――. "The *New York Times* 'Test' on American History," *Social Education,* Vol. VII (May 1943), pp. 195–200.

KELLER, CHARLES R. A talk given at the 45th Annual Convention of the National Association of Secondary School Principals in Detroit, Michigan, on February 11, 1961. Mimeographed.

National Education Association. *Report of the Committee of Ten on Secondary School Studies appointed at a meeting of the National Education Association July 9, 1892, with the Reports of the Conferences arranged by this Committee and held December 28–30, 1892.* Washington, D.C.: Government Printing Office, 1893.

Nevins, Allan. "American History for Americans," *New York Times Magazine*, May 3, 1942, p. 64.

New York Times, April 4, 1943 (More American history): July 24, 1963 (Dr. Wiesner).

Preliminary Statements by Chairmen of Committees of the National Education Association on the Reorganization of Secondary Education. U.S. Bureau of Education Bulletin No. 41. Washington, D.C.: U.S. Bureau of Education, 1916.

Report of the Committee on the Social Studies. . . . U.S. Bureau of Education Bulletin No. 28. Washington, D.C.: U.S. Bureau of Education, 1916.

Seignobos, Charles. *L'Histoire dans l'Enseignement Secondaire: La Conception Nouvelle de l'Histoire: La Méthode.* Paris: Librairie Armand Colin, 1906. Unpublished translation by Paul Lutz.

Tryon, Rolla M. *The Social Sciences as School Subjects,* Report of the Commission on the Social Studies, Part XI. New York: Scribner, 1935.

Wesley, Edgar B. (director). *American History in Schools and Colleges:* Report of the Committee on American History in Schools and Colleges of the American Historical Association, The Mississippi Valley Historical Association, and the National Council for the Social Studies. New York: Macmillan, 1944.

GENERAL METHODS

Cartwright, William H., and Watson, Richard L., Jr. (eds.). *Interpreting and Teaching American History.* Washington, D.C.: National Council for the Social Studies, 1961.

Johnson, Henry. *Teaching of History in Elementary and Secondary Schools with Applications to Allied Studies.* New York: Macmillan, 1940.

Lewenstein, Morris R. *Teaching Social Studies in Junior and Senior High Schools.* Chicago: Rand McNally, 1963.

Service Center for Teachers of History Pamphlets. New York: Macmillan, 1957–1964.

Thursfield, Richard E. (ed.). *The Study and Teaching of American History.* Washington, D.C.: National Council for the Social Studies, 1946.

Wesley, Edgar B., and Wronski, Stanley P. *Teaching Social Studies in High Schools.* Boston: Heath, 1958.

SOURCE METHOD

Barnes, Mary D. Sheldon. *Studies in General History.* Boston: Heath, 1891.

—— and BARNES, EARL. *Studies in American History.* Boston: Heath, 1891.

HART, ALBERT BUSHNELL (ed.). *American History Told by Contemporaries,* 5 vols. New York: Macmillan, 1897–1929.

—— and CHANNING, EDWARD (eds.). *American History Leaflets,* 34 vols. New York: Lovell, 1892–1902.

KEOHANE, ROBERT E. "The Great Debate Over the Source Method," *Social Education,* Vol. XIII (May 1949), pp. 212–218.

——. "Use of Primary Sources in United States History for High School Pupils," *School Review,* Vol. LIII (December 1945), pp. 580–587.

LANGLOIS, CHARLES V., and SEIGNOBOS, CHARLES. *Introduction to the Study of History.* London: Duckworth, 1898.

MACDONALD, WILLIAM (ed.). *Select Documents Illustrative of the History of the United States 1776–1861.* New York: Macmillan, 1897.

——. (ed.). *Select Statutes and Other Documents Illustrative of the History of the United States.* New York: Macmillan, 1903.

MCLAUGHLIN, A. C.; DODD, W. E.; JERNEGAN, M. W.; and SCOTT, A. P. *Source Problems in United States History.* New York: Harper, 1918.

Maynard's Historical Classic Readings, 10 nos. New York: Charles E. Merrill, 1890.

MEAD, EDWIN DOAK (ed.). *Old South Leaflets,* 125 nos. Boston: Directors of the Old South Work, 1883–1901.

New England History Teachers' Association. *Historical Sources in the Schools,* Report to the New England History Teachers' Association by Select Committee. New York: Macmillan, 1902.

ROBINSON, JAMES H.; CHEYNEY, EDWARD P.; HOWLAND, ARTHUR C.; and others (eds.). *Translations and Reprints from the Original Sources of History,* Department of History, University of Pennsylvania. Philadelphia: University of Pennsylvania Press, 1894–1907.

ABLE STUDENTS

COHEN, HELEN L. (ed.). *Educating Superior Students.* New York: American Book, 1935.

GAVIAN, RUTH WOOD (ed.). *The Social Education of the Academically Talented.* National Council for the Social Studies Curriculum Series No. 10, 1960.

GOLDBERG, MIRIAM L. "Recent Research on the Talented," *Teachers College Record,* Vol. LX (December 1958), pp. 150–163.

HENRY, NELSON B. (ed.). *The Education of Exceptional Children.* The

Forty-Ninth Yearbook of the National Society for the Study of Education. Chicago: University of Chicago Press, 1950.

————. (ed.). *Education for the Gifted*. The Fifty-Seventh Yearbook of the National Society for the Study of Education. Chicago: University of Chicago Press, 1958.

HOLLINGWORTH, LETA S. "The Founding of Public School 500: Speyer School," *Teachers College Record*, Vol. XXXVIII (November 1936), pp. 119–128.

————. *Gifted Children, Their Nature and Nurture*. New York: Macmillan, 1926.

KLEIN, MILTON M. *Social Studies for the Academically Talented Student in the Secondary School*. Washington, D.C.: National Education Association, 1960.

National Education Association, Research Division. "High School Methods With Superior Students," *Research Bulletin* 19, No. 4 (1941), pp. 156–197.

OSBURN, W. J., and BAHAN, BEN J. *Enriching the Curriculum for Gifted Children*. New York: Macmillan, 1931.

PASSOW, A. HARRY; GOLDBERG, MIRIAM; TANNENBAUM, ABRAHAM J.; and FRENCH, WILL. *Planning for Talented Youth*. New York: Bureau of Publications, Teachers College, Columbia, 1955.

TERMAN, LEWIS M. *The Intelligence of School Children*. Boston: Houghton Mifflin, 1919.

WITTY, PAUL (ed.). *The Gifted Child*. Boston: Heath, 1951.

TESTING

BRINKLEY, STERLING G. *Values of New Type Examinations in the High School* with Special Reference to History. New York: Teachers College, Columbia University, 1924.

College Entrance Examination Board. *Advanced Placement Program: Course Descriptions*. Princeton, N.J.: Educational Testing Service, 1960.

————. *Examination Questions in History*, 5 series. Boston: Ginn, 1905–1925.

————. *Your College Board Scores: Scholastic Aptitude Test, Achievement Tests*. [Princeton, N.J.] (pamphlet).

DEWEY, H. E. *Unit Tests in the Social Studies*. Yonkers-on-Hudson, N.Y.: World Book, 1941.

"Final Report and Recommendations of the Commission on History to the College Entrance Examination Board," *Social Studies*, Vol. XXVII (December 1936), pp. 546–566.

GIBBONS, ALICE N. *Tests in the Social Studies: A Record of a Testing Experience in Senior High School Social Studies,* National Council for the Social Studies Publication No. 3. Philadelphia: McKinley, 1929.

KELLEY, TRUMAN L., and KREY, A. C. *Tests and Measurements in the Social Sciences,* Report of the Commission on the Social Studies, Part IV. New York: Scribner, 1934.

MANUEL, HERSCHEL T. *Taking A Test How To Do Your Best.* Yonkers-on-Hudson, N.Y.: World Book, 1956.

RICHARDSON, M. W.; RUSSELL, J. T.; STALNAKER, J. M.; and THURSTONE, L. L. *Manual of Examination Methods.* Chicago: University of Chicago, 1933.

SHOEN, HARRIET H. *The History Examinations of the College Entrance Examination Board.* New York: The author, 1944.

STONE, ADOLPH. "The New York High School Regents Examinations in Social Studies." Unpublished doctoral project, Teachers College, Columbia University, New York, 1959.

STORMZAND, MARTIN JAMES. *American History Teaching and Testing.* New York: Macmillan, 1928.

The Teacher of History in the Secondary School, Papers Collated and and Issued by The Association of History Teachers of the Middle States and Maryland. Boston: Ginn.

THORNDIKE, ROBERT L., and HAGEN, ELIZABETH. *Measurement and Evaluation in Education and Psychology.* New York: John Wiley, 1961.

GRADING

BRIMM, R. P. "Thorny Problem—How Weight Student Marks in Honors Courses," *National Association of Secondary School Principals Bulletin,* Vol. XLV (April 1961), pp. 43–48.

"Does an Honors Course Penalize a Student?," *School Management,* Vol. V (March 1961), pp. 28–30.

TEXTBOOKS

ALEXANDER, ALBERT. "The Gray Flannel Cover on the American History Textbook," *Social Education,* Vol. XXIV (January 1960), pp. 11–14.

BEARD, CHARLES A., and BEARD, MARY R. *History of the United States.* New York: Macmillan, 1926.

FAULKNER, HAROLD UNDERWOOD, and KEPNER, TYLER. *America, Its History and People.* New York: Harper, 1934.

MUZZEY, DAVID SAVILLE. *An American History.* Boston: Ginn, 1911.

WIRTH, FREMONT P. *The Development of America.* Boston: American Book, 1936.

65